G

Godaesses

Deities

A GUIDE TO THE ANCIENT LGBTQIA+ WORLD

TOM LANTING

GREEN MAGIC

GREEN MAGIC
Seed Factory
Aller
Langport
Somerset
TA10 0QN
England
www.greenmagicpublishing.com

Designed and typeset by Carrigboy, Wells, UK.
www.carrigboy.co.uk

ISBN 978 1 915580 25 2

GREEN MAGIC

WITH LOVE TO:

My husband Iain, my parents and my brothers.

DEDICATED TO:

Forest, Eydie, River and Elodie.

Front cover art created by Suzie E Goose.

Artwork depicts a stylised representation of the Filipino deity Bathala. Here seen as both their aspects, male and female, with the earth as the belly. Where they touch are the stars with the sun and moon on either side.
The rainbow infinity symbol represents their ever-present and eternal love.

Contents

Prologue

Since coming out as a teenager and devoting myself to Paganism, I always enjoyed reading about ancient cultures and their beliefs. Though I grew up in a Christian Brothers' doctrine, I had a few amazing history teachers who weren't afraid to delve deeper into the spiritual realms of the old ways and explore the mythos before Christian influence.

I remembered reading about the Greek pantheon and their not-so-subtle sexual escapades and thinking, "how far society hit the reverse gear on open sexuality." From then on, I've become fascinated by looking at stories from the ancient world and how religion and sexuality were combined in stature and one's NATURAL path in life.

This book is designed primarily as an easy reference guide. A guide I would have loved as a teenager growing up, to develop a deeper understanding of not just Paganism but that who I was becoming was not something to shy away from, but something that has always been an intrinsic part of humanity and connecting to the cosmos full of deities that love, cherish and seek the greater LGBTQI+ community as conduits to this world.

I am sure if you take away more layers of cultures and their pantheons, corroded by modern institutions, that you will find a greater list of deities who would fit within the pages of this book. Some are distant memories with a name, obscured and hidden by millennia of occupation; some have traversed the vast oceans and found canonization and refuge in new religions.

The gods, goddesses and deities I have chosen are a mix of ones that still represent the LGBTQI+. Some are chosen as their stories and characteristics from a modern understanding of sexuality belong and deserve to be re-embraced into the LGBTQI+ pantheon. Lastly, some are included as they have always been there to protect and nurture our community.

I hope this book serves not just as a reference tool, but that it may tempt you to research an individual's mythos and stories to bring them to life in your own personal journey and spiritual exploration.

I have organised the book into continental groups to help show to whom we have always belonged. Some may now be almost invisible or blurred with age and but show that we have always had a place in the universe.

Inside I have included a few poems and prayers that I've written, as well as some translated traditional prayers.

Please take what you will, do your own research and enjoy finding out more about those who you find a connection with. Together we can re-embrace these wonderful gods and goddesses, as well as give back to them their fuller, richer identities.

Bright blessings on your journey.
TOM LANTING.

LGBTQI+ Identity and Importance in the Ancient World

The LGBTQI+ community has, in the last few thousand years, sat on the sidelines under the eyes of modern religions. These three main religions have spread hatred, fear and bigotry within their flocks, which has resulted in the way we are depicted as characters in books, movies and social media.

Thankfully the world is changing. We are finally receiving more rounded roles, and we are taking our places within society in roles never dreamed possible, even twenty years ago; and, more importantly, we are being accepted for who we are.

Within this book, the importance is to highlight our communities standing within the old religions around the world.

When we travel through time, and journey throughout the world, we see similar threads emerge. Before the Abrahamic orders of Islam, Judaism and Christianity, sexuality in general was not written as negative to human evolution. While in some cultures, life and all concerning elements were fluid and had no basis on whether you were good or bad; in some other cultures, such as Japan's Shintō, sexuality was in general a procreative duty.

Many ancient nations evolved to have a greater understanding of sexuality, so much so that they acknowledged up to seven sexes; this is seen not just within many of the Polynesian islands but also within Indigenous American tribes who assigned work according to their sex.

Perhaps one of the most interesting elements that shows itself is just how many deities who are creator spirits or sun gods that are seen as LGBTQI+. The concept of a creator being of both male and female sexuality is quite prevalent, especially within the island kingdoms of Asia, while gay/bi sun gods are quite commonplace worldwide.

The old world and its beliefs, many of which are still practised, had social structure and community at their heart. Sexuality didn't condemn you or force you to hide yourself. For the most part, society acknowledged and, in many cases, revered the LGBTQI+ community through priesthood and shamanism.

Now the old ways and their plethora of pantheons are becoming re-embraced by a new generation, we are starting to feel the shackles of the modern Abrahamic religions' oppression crumble. Our rights as humans are coming back; and with that, our relative safety in embracing our identities – we are placing a safe footing on our path to human, spiritual and sexual enlightenment.

As the world once again shifts, we are once again hearing the calls of the ancients. You are valuable, you are powerful, you have a voice. Remember why you are different and treasure the knowledge that comes with it.

Get up off the sidelines and remember.

Australia

The indigenous Australians (or Aboriginals) are the residents of the largest island continent and are to date the longest continuous culture. They have been the keepers of their land for over 60,000 years. Before the decimation that came with white colonisation, there were around 500 different tribes in existence and, according to the Australian Institute of Aboriginal and Torres Strait Islander Studies (AIATSIS), there are more than 250 indigenous languages, including 800 dialects.

Within such a rich and diverse people, it is natural that stories of their Dreamtime have both similarities as well as slight changes. Though most naturally change due to landscape, it is most notable in the stories of the transformative Rainbow Serpent.

THE RAINBOW SERPENT

Just as there are so many languages, there are many names for the serpent of creation and yet the stories remain similar which, considering the vastness of Australia, is rather impressive.

One of the main stories is that in the Dreaming of the Indigenous peoples of Australia, it was the Great Snake that created the earth as we see it, by winding, slithering and curling its way over the surface. Its movements created the mountains and oceans. From its great mouth spewed all the natural life that we have today.

In some stories, the Great Snake creates rules for the animals to follow, in order to become humans.

The Rainbow Serpent is seen as a creator but like all creators, if they are not happy with their work, they can destroy and rebuild. As a snake, its tales are of respect for its power and ability, but they are also valuable lessons never to fully be beguiled as, even for all good intentions, a snake is a snake and, well, we are food.

As a solo snake is virtually impossible to identify the sex by general characteristics alone, it's also not surprising that this has given rise in stories where the sexuality of one spirit changes. Characteristics can be equally peaceful, nurturing and healing and on the other side be strong, destructive and punishing.

The Great Rainbow Serpent God Ungud can be seen as transgender or as a non-binary entity.

Angamunggi was another name for the same spirit. Although generally observed as a male, he was believed to also have a womb.

Whether you choose these names or any other you are picking a powerful totem on creativity, nurturing and life-giving but also life-destroying. Their energies and abilities are a mix of what men's work and women's work was within tribal customs.

Currently, the oldest found rock art in Arnhem Land, Northern Territory, has been given an approximation of belonging to around the time of 30,000 BCE.

The sacred areas acknowledged by the ancestors are still highly sacred and respected, with the great snake having become a totem of unity, culture, community and representation of the Indigenous peoples across the world.

There is a large music festival held yearly in Victoria called the Rainbow Serpent Festival.

Within the LGBTQI+ community, the Serpent still embraces the names of two groups set up for health and welfare – Black Rainbow and First Nations Rainbow.

- Sexuality – Transsexual/non-binary.
- Feast Day – Any.
- Symbology – Water, rainbows.
- Colours – All colours.
- Animal – Snake.
- Vocation – Creation.
- Incense – Eucalyptus, tea-tree, wattle.
- Crystals – Opal, mookaite.
- Altar – To create a space to embrace the great snake, set up your meditation space/altar/etc with prisms that light can pass through (either candle, tea-light or LED).

Although you can use the oils comfortably in the home, if you are doing something outside then burn eucalyptus leaves to give an authentic and traditional cleanse which is used in indigenous ceremonies.

The Rainbow Serpent is a very beautiful and sacred spirit to call forward to awaken your creative abilities or when you are feeling a writer's block. Allow it to enter and push right through what is holding you back. A wonderful way to call upon its power is to have a writing pad/canvas/etc with your chosen colours and let your imagination go to work. Embrace its power and let your creativity/re-creativity emerge.

> *From the darkness I break through,*
> *slithering, sliding, gouging, upheaving.*
> *I created all you live on,*
> *I can transform or destroy.*
> *You are all that I breathed out.*
> *Be warned, though loving,*
> *I can breathe you back in.*

New Zealand

In New Zealand, Maoris are re-embracing their early beliefs, and with that a re-understanding or embracing of who they are as a people. Within Maori oral and written works, sexuality was nothing to shy away from, with many stories and songs written about all relationships.

Maori culture has a word, *takatāpui*, which is used to describe Maori couples in caring relationships and is embraced within the LGBT+ umbrella. It is a term dated well before English occupation, which enables us to understand that Maoris recognised other forms of relationships.

Although *takatāpui* is the general term, the Maori have others, but this is always the first word, i.e. bisexual is *takatāpui kaharua*; *takatāpui wahine ki tāne* or *takatāpui tāne ki wahine* is for trans man and trans woman; lesbian is *takatāpui wahine*.

Ira kora is a name given to people who don't identify, but the majority of sexualities (i.e. trans and intersex people) can all use the Maori term *irawhiti*.

Sadly, any stories that might have been in existence are either lost or have not been found yet, but stories such as *Hinemoa* and *Tūtānekai* do help us understand relationships and the written acknowledgment of multi-sexual relationships being just as important to Maori origins and culture.

Today in New Zealand, there is a massive push within Maori society to learn true identity and customs and re-embrace all sections of community, as done before colonisation.

Polynesia and the South Pacific

The people of the South Pacific were great travellers who eventually settled on most of the islands and chains within the great expanse of the Pacific Ocean. The islanders, while paying homage to the deities of their homeland, awakened the spirituality of the places they made home.

Having their foundations in what today is Taiwan and Melanesia, the islanders brought their understanding of sexuality with them. With many islands living happily with three sexes – some others, more.

In Tonga, the third sex is known as *fakeleití*; in Samoa, it is known as *fa'afafine*; while the fourth sex is known as *fa'afatama*. In French Polynesia, transgender males are known as *mahu* or *rae rae*. In Hawaii, the third sex is called *māhū*.

The cultural roles of the third and fourth sexes are very much a natural and traditionally vital part of society. Roles of these sexes include the taboo area of teaching about sex, as well as looking after and caring for the island's aged population.

Many of the islands have their own names, with myths and stories expressing society's values. Sadly, the only chain that has kept its stories intact from the ravages of Christian missionaries, colonisation and exploitation of its peoples and lands has been Hawaii. It is, however, due to Hawaii and fragments from intact Maori stories that historians can piece together how communal and all-encompassing the islanders were.

VANUATU

QAT

Most of the true nature of the deities within the pantheon of Vanuatu has disappeared. Qat remains within obscure context. Qat was a transmorphic god with the lower body of a man and the upper body of a shark. Though his main role now is as the protector of fishermen on their journeys to catch food for their families, he was/is a guardian and protector of homosexuality, who approves relationships among males.

- Sexuality – Gay.
- Feast Day – Unknown.
- Symbology – Fishing boats, fish, hook.
- Colours – Blue, turquoise and green.
- Crystals – Shell, aqua-marine, moonstone, ethically-sourced abalone, ethically-sourced coral.
- Animal – Shark.

- Vocation – Protecting fishermen on hunts. Patron of gay men.
- Incense – Frangipani and coconut.
- Altar –To connect with Qat, give your altar a watery energy by dressing it with a shimmering blue cloth and light a few white candles. Votives to place on your altar can be a fish, a hook, an image of a shark (whatever species you connect with) or a fishing boat. I find that although he is the protector of fishermen, he is a great guide to have on astral journeys or any difficult paths you are trying to traverse.

HAWAII

The 137 islands that make up Hawaii were inhabited by the travelling Polynesians. They are still rich in ancient lore that gives us a more intimate understanding of the entirety of the Polynesian South Pacific peoples, pre-colonisation. Out of this region, their stories have changed little. Even so, the entirety of human relationships is visible.

As the central pantheon of the Hawaiian pantheon came to the islands from other parts of Polynesia, they dwell in the main volcano, Kilauea.

Hawaii's legends and way of life help us understand the broader Pacific nations before Christianity's influence. It today reflects what was in island life.

Aloha.
We are lands of fragile beauty,
Of the sacred volcano and Hula
Ferns by our waist, plumeria by our neck and hair.
We love for love not for your sex.
Call to us on the breeze,
No matter what or who you are.
We are here.
Ohana.

WAHINEOME

Wahineomo (the Hawaiian Forest Goddesses), Hi'iaka (Hula, Magic Goddess) and human Hopoe all are represented as being in relationships at one time or another. Out of these, the saddest story is of bi Hi'iaka and her love, Hopoa. Pele the Volcano Goddess killed Hopoa with lava, as she suspected Hi'iaka of having an affair with her husband during one of her jealous tempers.

- Sexuality – Bisexual.
- Feast Day – Unknown.
- Symbology – Flowers and trees.
- Colours – Shades of greens, but all tropical colours.
- Crystal – Lava, peridot.
- Animal – Thrush.
- Vocation – Rainforest deity. Helper for environmental work.
- Incense – Sandalwood, hibiscus, plumeria, jasmine.

- Altar – Setting up an altar with green candles and green cloth works fine, but as Wahineome is a forest goddess, bring in tropical pinks, reds, yellows, etc. Whatever you feel connects to her. If you want, bring in a picture or two of rainforests. Call upon her when doing planetary energy work or for environmental issues.

HI'IAKA

Hi'iaka, though Hawaiian, was conceived in Tahiti but, as an egg, brought and incubated by Pele, her oldest sister. Under Pele's instructions, she was the first goddess to dance to hula – henceforth becoming its patron.

Though sexuality was in its very nature fluid, throughout the stories and journeys of Hi'iake there are numerous occasions where we can read of her *aikane* (same-sex) relationships – especially with Hopoe, a native human to these shores, who taught her the old dances and how to make *leis* (flower garlands).

- Sexuality – Bi-sexual/lesbian.
- Feast Day – Unknown.
- Symbology – The egg.
- Crystal – Egg shells, lava, ethically-sourced black coral, garnet.
- Colour – Red.
- Animal – Owls.

- Vocation – Patron Goddess of Hawaii, Storms, Medicine and the Hula.
- Incense – Lehua (myrtle family), sandalwood, hibiscus, jasmine, plumeria (frangipani).
- Altar –To set up a space for Hi'iaka is very simple. Use a red cloth, red candles and an egg. The egg can be a real one or a gemstone one, the magical usage is similar. To ask for Hi'iaka's help in healing, take the egg. If using a real egg, write your intention (or what needs to be healed, on who, etc) onto the shell. If it is a gemstone then write on with washable ink (the same thing). Use your time with Hi'iaka to focus on who needs help and where in/on their body the energy needs to go. Ask her to assist in the healing process.

As with all healing deities, don't ask for things that can't be undone, but instead for help to make the journey less painful and easier on the person.

After you are finished, it is up to you what to do with the egg. You are sending those intentions into action so you can either crack it on a rock, or else lose it in the waterways, or any other way you feel. The gemstone you can take to a waterway and wash the words off, envisioning the intention flowing and healing.

KAMAPUA'A

On the Hawaiian island of Maui, the Pig God Kamapua'a is Pele's husband. Nonetheless, he also had relationships with the bisexual god Limaloa. In many of the Island's stories, Kamapua'a is seen as a trickster but adolescent at heart. Not afraid to mix things up sexually, one of his stories tells of a time where Pele's brothers, Hi'iakaluna and Hiiakalalo, were harassing Kamapua'a; and so, to distract them, he summoned the Love God Lonoi to seduce them both.

Being born of Hawaii, Kamapua'a is an original deity of the islands.

- Sexuality – Bisexual.
- Feast Day – Unknown.
- Symbology – The kukui tree.
- Crystal – Rainbow moonstone.
- Colours – Red, turquoise and green.
- Animals – Hogs, wild boar and the reef triggerfish.
- Vocation – Fertility.
- Incense – Jasmine, sandalwood, honeysuckle, geranium, kukui oil.
- Altar – As Kamapua'a is both a fertility demigod as well as a healer of broken hearts, he is a wonderful deity to call forward when you need to find the love and ability to grow within.

Sacred moving water is important to cool what is negative, and hurtful fires still burn. So, instead of an altar, create a sacred space in your bathroom. Light your candles and allow the bathroom to turn into a space of dancing light. Focus on wounds that need to be addressed before you can grow. Turn your shower on; watching the candlelight hit the water like pure golden energy. Step inside. As you wash, envision yourself removing every negative toxin from your body, and these being washed away by the magical waters. Once you feel revitalised, turn the shower off and remove any last bits of water before you dry off.

Do this anytime you feel the inability to grow.

PAUOPALAE

Another story tells of the Fern Goddess Pauopalae and the Goddess Hi'iake in a lesbian relationship, while other stories offer a more polyamorous account of events.

Pauopalae started life coming from the islands' faerie realm, becoming an attendant to the Volcano Goddess Pele and her family but, as she was so loyal and had her own supernatural powers, she became a demigoddess. She protects all types of ferns on Hawaii's islands.

- Sexuality – Lesbian/polyamorous.
- Feast Day – Unknown.
- Symbology – Fern.
- Crystals – Green amethyst, rose quartz, peridot, citrine and chrysoprase.

- Colours – All shades of green.
- Animals – Bids, butterflies.
- Vocation – Guide, protector.
- Incense – Honeysuckle, gardenia, sandalwood.
- Altar – To invoke Pauopalae, give your altar a fresh tropical feel. She is a guide and may be called upon as such; remember her roots are in the original magical fae folk of the islands. Green candles, succulent incense and, if you are able to, bring in some ferns. If not, pictures of any type of fern or a fern grove may help bring focus to your mind.

Asia

Asia has a truly amazing number of LGBTQI+ deities – more so, trans figures. Many of the region's fundamental creator deities are indeed of both sexes. Asia has a fantastic diversity of beliefs and religions, spawned by a region of 44.58 million square kilometres, a diverse range of cultural identities and inter-traveling due to economic powers.

It does seem interesting that out of all continents, Asia isn't just the powerhouse of rainbow deities but, in particular, it is home to the largest array of trans beings.

BORNEO

MAHATALA-JATA

In Borneo, Mahatala-Jata is a trans deity who represents the tree, with him (Mahatala) and his sister (Jata) as combined, symbolising the upper and lower worlds. In the majority of myths surrounding this creator dual spirit, it is said that Mahatala is ruler of the upper world and lives above our world as a hornbill in the clouds; whereas Jata rules the underworld and lives in the water depths and is a great sea snake. Mahatala and Jata are connected by a stunning jewel that creates the rainbows we see in our world.

- Sexuality – Transsexual/non-binary.
- Feast Day – You could use the summer equinox to link to the upper world, and winter equinox to link to the underworld.
- Symbology – The great tree, rainbows.
- Crystals – Bumble bee jasper, coral jasper, diamond, rainbow moonstone, labradorite.
- Colours – Yellow, white, sea green, blue. All colours.
- Animals – The hornbill and sea snake.
- Vocation – Creator.
- Incense – Sandalwood and patchouli.
- Altar – To connect to the energies of Mahatala-Jata, I find that filling a bowl with water and lighting a yellow tea-light helps to combine the two aspects perfectly. Your altar you could keep neutral, apart from a rainbow image. I personally like to have a votive of a hornbill and a sea snake to symbolise them, but find your own way.

MENJAYA RAJA MANANG

The God/dess Menjaya Raja Manang of Borneo was the chief deity of the transgender shamans – the 'Manang Bali' principal healers. These shamans go through three main stages on their way to becoming true shamans, just as Menjaya did in order to heal his brother's wife.

Starting with dreams as young boys in which they see themselves as females, they gradually move from awakening shamans to becoming the Manang Bali, who take on female customs and clothing, as well as only having sexual relationships with men.

- Sexuality – Transsexual/non-binary.
- Feast Day – Unknown.
- Symbology – Unknown.
- Crystals – Septarian, rose quartz, amethyst.
- Colours – White, light blue, yellow.
- Animal – Elephant, snake, butterfly.
- Vocation – Healing, caring, compassion.
- Incense – All healing incenses.
- Altar – As only pieces about Menjaya are known, it allows a bit of flexibility. If you feel drawn to this deity, then rely on your own feelings. You may wish to simply settle for a healing altar with an elephant or butterfly as a totem, along with some rose quartz.

PHILIPPINES

The deities of Philippine indigenous culture have been misrepresented and confused since the Christian missions of Spanish occupation in 1565. For this reason, I have referenced Ikapate and Lakapati as separate entities.

There is an amazing re-awakening of these deities. They are being brought back to life by new generations through artwork and photography, their stories being re-told by groups set up like the Aswang Project.

BATHALA

Bathala (man and woman in one) is the creator of the universe. He is also known as the Great Caretaker, who looks after all life on earth. In the creation myth, Bathala came from the sky after feeling lonely and created all of life from a coconut tree. He is portrayed as gender androgynous.

- Sexuality – Non-binary.
- Feast Day – Unknown.
- Symbology – The coconut.
- Crystal – Clear quartz.
- Colours – All colours.
- Animal – Cockerel.
- Vocation – Creator of all.
- Incense – As a creator deity, choose herbs or oils to represent each element.
- Altar – To create a sacred space, go outside into nature. Something simple to do is to get a coconut and write/inscribe onto it what you would like help with. Leave your coconut over a 24-hour period, then crack it open. You can drain the water onto your garden, remove the inner white coconut flesh to create food balls for the birds and animals, then use the husks as small plant pots (air plants look amazing on them).

* Note – Please take care. If you are not sure how to open a coconut, it's best to ask someone or search online.

IKAPATE

Ikapate was the other half of the creator deity and she was a healer and protector of children, as well as a creator deity whose dual form/husband is Bathala. In Tagalog myth, it is Ikapate who gives Bathala a ball of clay from which he moulds the world and all on it. Loving her partner's work, Ikapate hung it up to admire it. So the earth is brought to life.

- Sexuality – Duel/non-binary.
- Feast Day – Unknown.
- Symbology – Clay, coconuts.
- Crystal – Clear quartz, rose quartz, amethyst.
- Colours – Green, light blue, yellow.
- Animal – Cockerel.
- Vocation – Co-creator.
- Incense – As dual creator with Bathala, use an even blend of herbs/oils from the elements.
- Altar – Find a space outside, if you prefer; especially a garden. I like to do a bit of spell work and gardening at the same time. Find a plant you want to grow and, before you do anything, write on the pot a simple word that carries your prayer. Give it a good soak before planting. When it comes to planting, use the entirety of the experience as a form of meditative state, so you are planting your desires and giving them the ability to grow and thrive. Take care and nurture your plant, while reminding yourself of what you have asked for.

LAKAPATI

Lakapati is considered to be one of the most understanding and nurturing of Philippine deities. Seen as intersex or hermaphrodite, she is the Goddess of Fertility, Prosperity, Healing and Agriculture.

- Sexuality – Intersex.
- Feast Day – Unknown, but celebrated at the beginning of and during harvest season.
- Symbology – Unhusked rice.
- Crystal – Moss agate.
- Colours – Greens, brown, yellow, blue.
- Animal – Carabao buffalo.
- Vocation – Fertility and agriculture.
- Incense – Sandalwood, patchouli and mint.
- Altar – As a deity of abundance and healing, a clean white altar is a good general start. If you have a garden, bring in some freshly cut flowers, herbs, etc, as an offering. If not, try some rice/corn/cereal in a bowl.

SIDAPA AND BULAN

In some Philippine myths, Sidapa is the God of Death, who lives on Mt. Madjaas. It is said that he fell in love with the beautiful youth, the Moon God Bulan, and after time courting him, the two moved into Sidapa's mountain home, where they still live. Bulan today is seen as the patron god of homosexuality.

SIDAPA

- Sexuality – Gay.
- Feast Day – Unknown.
- Symbology – A tree (which measures lifespans).
- Crystals – Black obsidian, tourmaline.
- Colours – Black, gold.
- Animals – Black bats, crows, black butterflies.
- Vocation – Caretaker of the dead and protector of the ill and dying.
- Incense – Any herbs or oils that you would usually use for spirit work and/or healing the sick.
- Altar – A dark altar with gold candles seems to work well. If you use a crystal ball or scrying obsidian then you can always ask for Sidapa's help and guidance in protecting you. If you astral travel, you can ask for his assistance to protect your body. If you are calling on him to either guide a person's way to the otherworld, or to ask for a person who is very ill to get better, then bring in more healing and nurturing herbs.

BULAN

- Sexuality – Gay.
- Feast Day – Unknown.
- Symbology – The moon, lotus, water hyacinth.
- Crystals – Moonstone, obsidian.
- Colours – White/ silver, black.
- Animal – Crane.
- Vocation – The moon, homosexuality.

- Incense – Jasmine, bergamot, lotus (any lunar herbs or oils).
- Altar – You can set up an altar to Bulan by simply using all white cloth and candles. Place your altar so that you can see and feel the moon. Place a silver/aluminium bowl filled with water to reflect the moon's light.

MAKAPATAG-MALAON

Makapatag-Malaon in Waray mythology is the simultaneously half-male/half-female great creator. They have very separate attributes. Makapatag is fearsome in nature; as the leveller, his power is destructive. On the flip side, Malaon the ancient one is serene and gentle by nature.

*Note: very little is known about this deity.

- Sexuality – Dual/intersex/non-binary.
- Feast Day – Unknown.
- Symbology – I like to use scales or a ying yang symbol to show the quality and equal duality of their nature.
- Crystals – Lava, tektite, opal.
- Colours – Unknown but, again, go with two colours on opposite spectrums.
- Animal – Unknown but, as a creator, go to what you are drawn to.
- Vocation – Creator.

- Incense – Create one by mixing herbs representing the elements.
- Altar – I would recommend, if drawn to this dual deity, that you go with your instinct. So little is known that it allows you to create your own relationship.

China

Ancient Chinese writings are full of LGBTQI+ references. From dragons that like to have sex with older men, to animal spirits and fairies that choose same-sex human partners. Take a small look into Imperial history, where you will find examples of male concubines for royal pleasure – Emperor Ai and many others are notably written as enjoying their male concubines whilst also having wives.

TU ER SHEN

Tu Er Shen is involved with gay affairs of love and relationships in the Taoist belief. In China, this Daoist deity of gay men and relationships was also known as the Rabbit God.

Originally a human, he was a soldier who was secretly in love with another soldier. After being caught spying on him while showering, his commanding officer had Tu Er Shen put to death. Tu Er Shen returned as a vision in a dream of a local man, telling him that he had been turned into a god for his unjust death.

Throughout the history of China, Tu Er Shen's followers have met with many forms of adversity, even being banned by some Emperors but, thanks to multimedia, Tu Er Shen is still with us and gaining a new following, with movies like *Kiss of the Rabbit God*.

As recently as 2006, a temple to Tu Er Shen was built in New Taipei, Taiwan. It is frequently visited by the gay Taiwanese community, searching for their Mr Right.

- Sexuality – Gay.
- Feast Day – Unknown.
- Symbology – Rabbit.
- Crystals – Carnelian, rose quartz, garnet.
- Colours – Red and gold.
- Animal – Rabbit.
- Vocation – Gay love and relationships.
- Incense – Nag Champa always works well, though I personally like to use jasmine and orange – but create one that feels right to your connection.
- Altar – I like to keep rabbits (statues) in the home as a way to embrace his energies. When working directly, I like to bring a statue onto the altar with a red cloth and gold candles. Even if you're not actually doing anything, it's nice just to know he's there watching over you.

> *I call upon you Tu Er Shen,*
> *Beloved of mortal gay men.*
> *I seek only happiness in my relationship,*
> *May it be honest and true.*

THE JADE RABBIT

The Jade Rabbit or Moon Rabbit is a very popular story. The Jade Rabbit is a companion to the Moon Goddess, Chang'e. He and his pestle of healing herbs can be seen every August on the Rabbit Full Moon. He frequently changes from male to female and is also known as a healer of mortals.

- Sexuality – Dual aspect/intersex.
- Feast Day – Rabbit Moon and the Mid-autumn Festival or Moon Festival, 15th day of the 8th month of the lunar calendar.
- Symbology – Moon, rabbit, pestle & mortar.
- Crystal – Jade.
- Colour – Jade green.
- Animal – Rabbit.
- Vocation – Healing, magical herb lore. Selflessness. All areas of generosity.
- Incense – You can use any, although all healing blends will do.
- Altar – The Jade Rabbit is a creature of generosity and devotion. A great time to call on him is whenever you need healing or are sending it to another. You can always start with a green cloth, silver candles, your lit incense and a bowl of water. Take a piece of jade and, in the candlelight, hold it tight in your palms. Focus on who or what you are wishing health towards. Once you feel ready, open your hands and show the jade to the moon candles. Hover it over the incense and then place it into the bowl.

Remember to thank the Jade Rabbit. Love and giving with your heart is the Rabbit's motto.

Rabbit, rabbit of sacred jade,
Mix in your pestle a mixture pure
Of love, joy, healing and strength,
To spread upon the earth.
Companion to Chang'e,
Show your love, generosity and compassion
Through how I treat those who disrespect me.

Japan

In the Shintō main pantheon structure, you will not find LGBT out deities (kami), but they are there in Shintō offshoots. As a belief structure principled on nature, without any singular text or format, Shintō is as old as Japan. I'm sure, on closer inspection, you may find more LGBT+ kami that are waiting for their voices to be heard again.

> *The mountain sits in solitude.*
> *The crane flies gently above the mountain.*
> *Fox changes form.*

SHUDŌ DAIMYŌJIN

Shudō is the folk deity of homosexuality and same-sex love.

- Sexuality – Gay.
- Feast Days – 1st January, New Year's Day can be used. Valentine's Day on 14th February can be a great day to seek attract love.
- Symbology – The crane.
- Crystals – Garnet, clear quartz.
- Colours – Red, white.
- Animal – The Crane.
- Vocation – Homosexuality, love.

- Incense – Jasmine, sandalwood, cherry, wisteria, rose.
- Altar – As a deity of love, decorate your altar in a way that shows beauty. If you want, you could maybe use the rainbow flag or your own appropriate flag as a cloth – after all, the altar reflects you also.

Choose your colour-coded candles and incense. If you are seeking love or trying to find love within yourself then ask for guidance, close your eyes and let the candles' light envelop you.

ŌYAMAKUHI NO KAMI

Ōyamakuhi no Kami is a transgender mountain deity of industry, good health and childbearing. They are also the guardians of Tokyo.

- Sexuality – Transsexual.
- Feast Day – 1st January, New Year's Day.
- Symbology – Mountains.
- Crystals – All raw natural pieces.
- Colours – Red, brown, white, blue and green.
- Animals – Dragon, carp.
- Vocation – Homosexuality, childbirth and industry.
- Incense – Earthy elements. I recommend magnolia or cherry.
- Altar – Keep it simple and natural with brown and greens. Incorporate cherry blossoms in the spring or if you have a bonsai tree then place it on the altar. If

not, then a picture of a Japanese mountain scene to focus on will do perfectly.

INARI

Inari is the deity of agriculture and industry and is one of the principal kami of Shintō. Inari is sometimes male, sometimes female, sometimes androgynous.

As a deity who is patron of swordsmanship and prosperity, Inari can also be seen as a shapeshifting fox and many statues of Inari situated at temples are of a giant fox with a sword in mount.

- Sexuality – Intersex.
- Feast Days – 6th February and the week of the November full moon.
- Crystals – Copper, bronze, aluminium (any metals used in construction).
- Symbology – Swords and rice.
- Colours – Red, gold.
- Animal – The fox.
- *Anytime I go for a walk at night I always make sure I have food to feed the foxes near me. They may not be Inari, but you never know.
- Vocation – Craftspeople, success and progress.
- Incense – Mint, patchouli, clove and cinnamon.
- Altar – When setting up an altar to the Inari, I always like to be a bit decedent. Try using red or gold velvet for a cloth, with red candles. For any accompanying pieces for the altar, use gold/brass/chrome (shiny metals).

One of the most important days in Shintō is New Year's Day, 1st January. It is believed that on this day the deities' spirits fill the home. Why not make it into a special day to invoke any or all of the deities mentioned above? Break out a bottle of saki, or perhaps a Japanese beer such as Asahi, to give as a libation.

The Middle East

At the height of its power, the Middle East flourished as a home where magic, science, astronomy and mathematics became highly advanced and intertwined. Before the Eastern branches of the Abrahamic faiths started to erode the cultures, their deities were as advanced in wisdom and spirituality as the people were in their understanding of the universe.

MESOPOTAMIA

Ancient Mesopotamia in Greek means 'between two rivers' which is quite apt as it lay between the mighty Euphrates and Tigris rivers in an area that is modern-day Iraq, Iran, Syria and Kuwait, as well as parts of Turkey.

An ancient land, it bore the earliest cities, whilst giving us early governance, as well as science, maths and astronomy.

It was home to the Babylonians, Assyrians and Sumerian peoples.

Our lady mighty queen,
Queen of the heavens, star of the sea,
you are the morning star that brings warmth,

you who are always ready for battle.
You welcome us as 'we',
you who sees our soul, not skin.
Guide me; help me be, that who I truly am.

ATTART/ASHTART/ASTARTE/ RA-ASTARTE

Star of the Sea

Astarte is the mother of all mothers in Middle Eastern to Western cultures.

Not to be confused with Ishtar, the cult of Astarte, though Western Semitic, encompassed a great deal of the then travelled world, spreading even into Britain (one from Corbridge, Northumberland, sits in the Tullie House Museum).

Her origins come from the Canaanites and her homes were on the sea ports of the Mediterranean – Elat, Sidat and Tyre – where they erected obelisks to her. A well-travelled goddess, she was worshipped far and wide in different guises. In Egypt, she was Qatesh (Anat), as well as becoming or being absorbed into the Greek Aphrodite.

- Sexuality – Cis.
- Feast Day – 1st January.
- Symbology – The 16-pointed star, the planet Venus, the egg, solar disc and lunar disc.
- Colour – Red.
- Crystals – Emerald, rose quartz.

- Animals – Lion, Sphinx, dove and horse.
- Vocation – She was the Goddess of Love, Sex, War and Hunting.
- Incense – Copal, amber, frankincense.
- Altar – When setting up an altar, I like to add a crystal obelisk in the centre with red candles around it. Keeping a libation of bread and honey for her that can be fed to the birds afterwards.

INANNA

QUEEN OF THE HEAVENS

(Refer to Ishtar)

Inanna was a goddess from Sumer and was worshipped in Mesopotamia where her biggest temple was in the city of Urak. Within her sacred temples were her priests or 'Gala' who were 3rd gender, linking to the fact that Inanna could change a person's sex. Many inscriptions, artworks and stories that still exist help us to see and understand both her and a liberal Sumer.

Inanna/Ishtar is regarded by academics as the most important goddess in the Mesopotamian world, in all periods. There are many fantastic myths and hymns about her and her ability to change her priests' sexes. One such book for fantastic reference is *Sag Su Bal*. The Head-Overturning Rite has finally been translated into English by author, Steff V Scott.

- Sexuality – Androgynous.
- Feast Days –
  - 1st January: Vernal and autumnal equinox, the Sacred Mace Ceremony (the full moon directly after the vernal equinox), the month of Kin-Inanna (end of August to early September, leading to the autumnal equinox).
  - 20th–21st March: Sumerian festival celebrating the return of Dumuzi (God of Life and Death) from the underworld to be with Inanna (Goddess of Life) for the verdant part of the year.
  - 30th April–2nd May: Feast of Sacred Marriage honouring the goddess/god as Inanna and Dumuzi (both the vernal and autumnal equinoxes are sacred times of worship for her).
- Symbology – The knot of Inanna, the crescent moon, the 8-pointed star, pomegranates, rainbows, Venus.
- Colours – Lapis lazuli, a rainbow or prism's spectrum, carnelian red, black and white.
- Crystals – Carnelian, lapis lazuli.
- Animal – Owls.
- Vocation – Goddess of Love, Kinship, Warfare and Battle. Fertility, sex.
- Incense – Storax, sandalwood, cedarwood and amber.
- Altar – A clean, simple space. I generally like to keep an owl statue out and simply light a candle and some incense. If you are making an offering, make your own pomegranate and rosewater drink. Use it afterwards as a libation.

* Please read the information on Ishtar, as well as Astarte. These three figures, though different, have throughout their time within human societies been seen as separate from, as well as interchangeable with, one another.

BABYLON

ISHTAR (SEE ALSO INANNA)

Ishtar from Babylonia could supernaturally change her male priests' sex to female. This sacred deity of Mesopotamia and Sumer has many fascinating hymns and scripts relating to her which reveal a culture that had a great gender-fluid/trans understanding. Ishtar later became a popular goddess in Egypt under the name Astaroth, or the more Hellenised name Astarte. Though they shared many traits and opposed in others, she can be seen depicted as androgynous.

- Sexuality – Androgynous.
- Feast Day – Fridays.
- Symbology – Dove, Star of Ishtar, bow & arrows, the moon, Venus.
- Colours – Carnelian red, white and black/lapiz blue.
- Crystals – Lapis lazuli, rose quartz and carnelian.
- Animals – Lions, bulls, dogs, snakes and doves.
- Vocation – Fertility, love, sex and war.
- Incense – Storax, amber, rose, cedarwood and sandalwood.
- Altar – As a general guidance, I like to create an altar with a black or silver cloth to represent the night or moon. Place a glass/crystal bowl of water with a carnelian in the centre.

The animal is your choice. As I work more with snake deities, I always have a snake statue around, but work with whichever animal you feel more connected to. Always be quite sure of your intention here as she is a dual-action goddess. You don't want to get love and war mixed up in any format.

GILGAMESH

The King of Urik in Mesopotamia was the son of the Goddess Ninsumun and a priest king named Lugalbanda.

We know a lot about Gilgamesh as the Sumerians wrote a great epic (the first great epic) about him, obviously called *The Epic of Gilgamesh*. Here it is plain to read about the relationship he had with what we would today class as a soulmate.

His relationship with the warrior and wild man Enkidu was recorded as just that, with even the purpose of him being born to be a completion of Gilgamesh: "Now go and create double for Gilgamesh, his second self, a man who equals his strength and courage, a man who matches his stormy heart" –*The Epic of Gilgamesh, Book 1*.

This relationship was even foretold by his mother: "A strong partner will come to you and you will love him as your wife." As the epic progresses, we see how they positively change each other, as a good relationship does. Even when Enkidu dies, we see the weakened figure of a lover who sets off to find immortality.

- Sexuality – Bisexual.

- Feast Days – Whenever you wish.
- Symbology – Sword.
- Colours – Gold, red, blue.
- Animals – The bull, lions.
- Vocation – Bravery, travelling, wisdom.
- Incense – Myrrh, amber.
- Alter – An altar here can very much be how you like. Perhaps a gold cloth representing him as a god, or purple as a king? What is your purpose? Either way, if seeking strength and wisdom then you may like to have statue of a lion or a bull to symbolise those qualities.

JUDAEA

The traditional area of Judaea was in ancient Palestine. It covered the hills of Judaea or Her Yehuda.

MIRYAM

Miryam/Mary – Hebrew. You may wonder why I'm adding a biblical figure here, but there is merit to her being here. As a later adaptation to the Mesopotamian Goddess Inanna, Hecate through to Isis then Aphrodite, Mary is the latest incarnation of a very ancient goddess. Mother deities have always been a port of safety and security to the LGBTQI+ community. Mary is no different.

Though many would acknowledge that 'virgin' in Hebrew ('alma') just meant 'young woman', the modern concept of virginity might be extremely flawed.

As Christianity moved around the world, Mary went with it. She has in many countries been given her own standing as well as being worshipped again in her goddess form. Mary's feast days are many, as there are now many branches of beliefs, but Mary's ability to be seen and heard further points to her sacred divine blood, as does her queenship.

- Sexuality – Cis.
- Feast Days – The month of May. Mary's birthday, 8th September.
- Symbology – The pansy, almond, olive, fleur-de-lys, rose, palm leaf.
- Colours – Blue, white.
- Crystals – Rose quartz, opal.
- Animal – Dove.
- Vocation – Mothering, nurturing, protection of those who feel lost and alone.
- Incense – Frankincense, rose, benzoin, monkshood.
- Altar – You can readily buy candles dedicated to the Virgin Mary, but you can create a nice simple altar with a blue cloth and white candles. In general, if you don't like the Christianised statues, get a lovely figure or picture of a dove. As Miryam/Mary is denoted as a queen of heaven, I tend to find that gold (coloured) altar tools work well here.

LILITH

Lilith was, in Abrahamic lore, the first. It was she who came before Adam and was made as a pure individual, equal to Adam. When she left Eden, in her story, to many, Lilith became more of a demon; whereas Eve became the readymade obedient and lesser human that Adam wanted. The fact that Lilith left, not wanting to be lesser than Adam, as well as wanting to have sex face-to-face, had her turned into a goddess of prostitutes and the evils of sexuality.

Lilith is not just a goddess of nurturing for children and childbirth but also a goddess of the pure love of sexuality. It is in this form that she becomes a relevant goddess and protector of not just the LGBTQI+ community but also to everyone willing to love and embrace their sexuality and not let others keep them from their true selves.

To give a full picture of her in religious texts, Lilith is also seen as a demon that sends men sexual dreams, leading in stealing their semen, as well as later a murderer of children.

Today Lilith has become an ambassador to the destitute and people from violent backgrounds (i.e. protector of child welfare and battered wives) but she has also become a goddess that the LGBTQI+ community can turn to for safety and nurture.

Lilith is for all intents and purposes the most changeable of the goddesses/deities in this book, as on one side she is a figure of fear and hate, but on the other side she is also a figure of compassion, showcasing her treatment by a god and a man.

- Sexuality – Cis.
- Feast Day – 24th October: Her defiance of Adam and leaving the Garden of Eden.
- Symbology – Apple.
- Crystal – Bloodstone.
- Colours – Red, black.
- Animals – Snake, owl.
- Vocation – Motherhood, protector of victims of spousal abuse, sexuality.
- Incense – Frankincense, apple, rose, myrrh.
- Altar – I find that an altar to Lillith needs to be simple and clean, just like your intentions with her. Mix perhaps some myrrh and rose together to strengthen emotions, especially if you are seeking a correct course of justice. Though all deities are of free mind, Lilith is that wee bit more so. Ask for her help. NEVER demand her help – you might not like the outcome.

Africa

Africa is such a great and ancient continent, considered the birthplace of mankind. Sadly, I have only been able to work with ancient Egyptian mythology here, though I do include some from West Africa which, as we see later, travelled through slavery to the Americas. I'm sure that if we scraped deeper into the heart of Africa there would be many more, BUT as new religions took over and eradicated the old ways, they removed elements that contradict the straight cis narrative.

EGYPT

In Egypt, the story of Set and Horus and their semen is one of the closest LGBT+ concepts, though Isis is also considered a natural ally and in some stories is seen in a form of relationship with the Scorpion Goddess Wadjet, as well her very own sister, Nephthys. The Nile Fertility Gods Wadj-wer and Hapy are usually seen with breasts.

TEMU/ATUM – EGYPT

The first of all deities in Egypt was Atum. Like many origin deities, they are of both sexes. As Atum is the very first, they gave birth to him/themself and through their own semen or a sneeze (debatable) they gave birth to two children, Shu and Tefnut.

- Sexuality – Dual. They.
- Feast Day – 23rd September.
- Symbology – The ankh, man, a staff.
- Crystals – Pyrite, opal, peacock ore.
- Colours – As with the beginning of creation, go with the colour that comes to mind, or a rainbow or prism spectrum.
- Animals – The ram, lizards, bull, snake, scarab beetle, Egyptian mongoose, as well as an ape and later the fish.
- Vocation – New life, new beginnings, creation. Lord of two lands.
- Incense – Amber, frankincense, lotus.
- Altar – A nice gold mirrored cloth that reflects the light always goes well with a solitary ankh in the centre with two pillar candles. If you prefer, you can always go with a scarab. Atum is a great one to call on for ANY new beginnings and is a great help in pushing or driving momentum.

Just like Atum, you don't need anyone else to give birth to your idea. You sometimes just need that light switched on.

HAPI – EGYPT

An intersex deity of the Nile. In most depictions of them, they have a male body with breasts, a pregnant belly, a beard and a penis.

- Feast Day – 28th September. Hapi was always worshipped at the annual food inundation, when the Nile was at its peak.
- Sexuality – Intersex.
- Symbology – Lotus crown, the Nile, the papyrus and lotus.
- Crystal – Lapis lazuli.
- Colours – blue and green.
- Animal – Crocodile
- Vocation – God of the annual floods. Fertility of land and all creatures.
- Incense – Lotus.
- Altar – Hapi is a wonderful deity to ask for help to grow ideas or seek progress when you feel at an end. If you can't find a lotus incense then work with an incense that you connect growth with. You could use a blue or green cloth with candles of the same colour so that when you light the flame, you may envision the light of the sun bringing warmth to your endeavours, and the river of the Nile overflowing into the driest areas of your thought processes.

Blessed Hapi,
They who give life to the sacred Nile,
Divine being of both roles.
May your totality give acceptance,
And love all others.

ASET/ISIS – EGYPT

As a mother goddess and protector of the downtrodden, Isis has long been the refuge for the LGBT+ community. Her temple priests were by most historical accounts gay as many Goddesses in history have had.

- Sexuality – Cis.
- Feast Days –
  - 5th March: Navigium Isidis – Honouring Isis as Lady of the Moon.
  - 23rd March: Festival of Isis.
  - 14th May: The Festival of Isis the Merciful. Also on this day is the Night of the Teardrops of Isis.
  - 16th May is the Festival of Isis as Giver of Life.
  - 17th May: A day to mark the Sorrows of Isis.
  - 23rd June: Celebrates the Rites of Isis and Osiris.
  - 17th July: The birthday of Isis.
  - 12th August: Festival of the Lights.
  - 7th October: The Feast of the Going Forth of Isis.
  - 31st October–3rd November: The Isia of Isis is held. The Mysteries of Osiris are also held during this period. It honours Osiris' death, dismemberment and resurrection by Isis.
  - 1st November: Marks her search for the scattered parts of his body, and putting her husband's body back together.
  - 22nd December: Day of the Mysteries of Isis.
  - 30th December: The Nativity of Isis.
- Apart from these sacred dates, every full moon is a powerful time to commune with her.

- Symbology – The thet/tyet or Knot of Isis, a throne.
- Crystals – Lapis lazuli, malachite, amethyst, desert rose, carnelian.
- Colours – Red, turquoise and green.
- Animals – The kite, vulture, cow, scorpion and snake.
- Vocation – Magic, motherhood, seafaring.
- Incense – Lotus, rose, frankincense, myrrh.
- Altar – I always have a little space somewhere set up for Isis. Arrange a turquoise or red cloth with a few green candles. Have your mix of incense ready to burn and, if you're good at moulding, maybe create her knot out of air-dry clay, or make a throne to sit on the altar. If not, a statue of her will more than do, and sprinkle it with roses.

Praise to you, Isis, the Great One,
The mother of Horus, Lady of Heaven,
Mistress and queen of the gods.
You are the First Royal Spouse of Osiris,
The supreme overseer of the Golden Ones in the
temples,
The eldest son, firstborn of Geb.
Praise to you, Isis, the Great One,
The mother of Horus, Lady of Heaven,
Mistress and queen of the gods.
You are the First Royal Spouse of Osiris,
The Bull, the Lion who overthrows all his enemies,
The lord and ruler of eternity.
Praise to you, Isis, the Great One,
The mother of Horus, Lady of Heaven,
Mistress and queen of the gods.

You are the First Elect One of Osiris,
The perfect youth who performs slaughter among the
*   disaffected*
of the Two Lands.
Praise to you, Isis, the Great One,
The mother of Horus, Lady of Heaven,
Mistress and queen of the gods.
You are the First Royal Spouse of Osiris,
One who protects her brother and watches over the
*   weary-of-heart.*
Praise to you, Isis, the Great One,
God's mother, Lady of Heaven,
Mistress and queen of the gods.
You are the First Royal Spouse of Osiris,
The Eternal One rejuvenating himself, who raised up
*   Eternity:*
You are with him in the Temple (of Philae).
Praise to you, Isis, the Great One,
God's mother, Lady of Heaven,
Mistress and queen of the gods.

– This hymn is inscribed in hieroglyphs on the rear wall of the Temple of Isis at Philae, circa 300 BCE.

SETH, HORUS AND THOTH – EGYPT

I am placing these three gods together to showcase the relationship between them. In ancient tales, Horus and Seth are depicted in a form of bonding one way or another.

Seth is one of the oldest Egyptian deities and so has many diverse roles and animals associated with him as his roles changed. On one side he was a god of chaos but, as evening came, he journeyed every night with Ra to keep Apep from destroying everything. Seth shows that organised, or planned, chaos is not a bad thing as it can create new opportunities. But outright chaos and destruction is never positive.

In the union between them, Thoth is born from Seth's forehead by Horus' semen. Other accounts of the story include sexual abuse which is more complicated with a lettuce with semen that creates birth after being eaten. Whichever way you read the story it says a lot about sexuality within Egypt.

Though other forms of sex may have been accepted. The role of the people within that relationship may have helped in roles within the home and outside.

You can read within this family the unifying of Upper & Lower Egypt through (and bringing with it) wisdom.

SUTEKH/SET/SETH

- Sexuality – Straight.
- Feast Days –
    - 13th August: The day of battle between Set and Horus.
    - 16th July: Set's birthday.
    - 14th August: Day of peace between Set and Horus.
- Symbology – The 'was' sceptre.
- Crystal – Carnelian.

- Colours – Red, black and gold.
- Animal – The kite, vulture, cow, scorpion and snake.
- Vocation – Earthquakes, eclipses, deserts, foreign lands, Protector of Ra.
- Incense – Liquorice, orris root, musk.
- Altar – Seth is not the most relaxed deity to work with, having a temper that can be volatile, but he is a great one to call on for strength to overcome fear, removal of obstacles (take as you wish), but also for the study of astral connection. Set out a space, dark and safe. Place a few candles in the above colours. If you like a statue, then place him there or, if you prefer, work with him using a picture of him in any of his animal forms.

HERU/HORUS

Horus is the child of Isis and Osiris, as well the nephew of Set. He was a beloved god of the Egyptians and still very much revered today. Born on the 25th of December as a SUN GOD, he is a basis of the Christians' Jesus.

His eyes represented the sun (right eye) and the moon (left eye).

- Sexuality – Straight.
- Feast Days –
  ○ 13th August: Day of battle between Horus and Set.
  ○ 14th August: Day of peace between Horus and Set.

- ○ 31st August: The white crown is received by Horus.
- ○ 25th December: The birth of Horus (child of Isis and Osiris).
- ○ 13th June: Horus the beloved celebrations.
- Symbology – The Eye of Horus.
- Crystals – Malachite, citrine, gold.
- Colour – Green.
- Animal – Falcon.
- Vocation – Truth, light and victory. God of the Sky, Moon and Sun.
- Incense – Chamomile, star anise, Frankincense.
- Altar – Set up a space by a window (or outside) with a silver and a gold candle to represent the sun and moon and place a statue or an Eye of Horus in the centre. Horus is a great deity to help you see the truth and find the right answers. I particularly like to place some chamomile oil on my third eye.

Tehuty/Thoth

Thoth is the God of Wisdom and Knowledge who brought the gift of hieroglyphics to the people of Egypt. He was also a lunar god as well as a god of maths and science.

Thoth was married to the Goddess of Law and Upholder of Balance, Ma'at.

- Sexuality – Straight.
- Feast Days –
  - ○ 6th August: Festival of Thoth.
  - ○ 20th August: Thoth orders the Eye of Horus be healed.

- ○ 14th December: Celebrates the day Thoth sends Sekhmet and Bast to guide Egypt.
- Symbology – Moon disk, a stylus and scribe's palette.
- Crystal – Emerald.
- Colours – Blue, silver/white.
- Animals – Baboon and ibis.
- Vocation – Wisdom, the written word and the moon.
- Incense – Papyrus.
- Altar – To this god of words, I like to use my writing space. Not an elegant or classy altar – but your writing, or work desk, is a great altar. It is always set up. I keep a statue of an ibis by my pens. It's a great way to acknowledge his wisdom every day.

Amun Re/Ra-Raet Tawy/Raet

The Egyptian Sun God had a female counterpart. Though much is unknown about Raet, the general consensus is that they are one and the same, though in later dynasties she became her own form.

- Sexuality – Non binary
- Feast Days –
  - ○ 6th August: Festival of Ra.
  - ○ 26th August: The jubilation of the heart.
  - ○ 31st October: Feast of Ra.
  - ○ 16th December: Ra is raised up by the hands of Ptah (creator god).
  - ○ 4th January: Celebrates the day of Raet and Nut heading south.
  - ○ 4th March: Feast of Ra on his barge.
  - ○ 2nd April: The day of Joy of Ennead.

- 26th May: The receiving of Ra.
- 16th June: Feast of Raet.
- 13th July: Birthday of Ra.
- Symbology – Sun disc, vulture feathers.
- Crystal – Carnelian.
- Colours – Red, yellow.
- Animal – Cow.
- Vocation – Sun Goddess, great mother.
- Incense – Chamomile, lotus, amber.
- Altar – You may like to invoke Raet at the same time as Ra, within their duality. Use a red cloth and yellow candles. If it's sunny, take it outside and make an offering of chamomile flowers, or plant chamomile in the lawn in her name.

WEST AFRICAN YORUBA PEOPLE

Inle

Inle is the god sacred to Nigeria's River Erinle, which is the sacred home to the I. Inle is a god of the in-between, he dwells in the area between fresh and seawater and so is at home hunting in the sea, as well as on land.

Inle is known as a healer and physician to the gods, regularly depicted as a young man with a snake coiled round him and long flowing hair. He is the protector and guardian of gay, lesbian, bi and trans people.

Like many of the Yoruba deities, they followed their enslaved people on the journey to the Caribbean and Americas as central figures in Voodoo.

- Feast Day – 29th September.
- Symbology – Cowrie shells, beautiful bird feathers, coral, hook, dagger, fish, staff. A snake trident.
- Crystals – Coral, shells, pearls, African opal.
- Colours – Sea green, blue, turquoise, white, coral, pink, yellow.
- Animals – He has a fond preference for pure white animals. He also loves rams and pigeons.
- Vocations – Homosexuality, doctors & nurses as well as all other healers, hunting.
- Incense – Orange, verbena, basil.
- Altar – Create a space using shells and pebbles from a river, lake or the sea. Make sure it's clean and tidy, ensuring you use some of his favourite colours for candles.

Call on Inle for help with healing for yourself or another person.

He loves fish, so I tend to find that offerings or votives of fish attract his attention.

Mawu-Lisa

Mawu-Lisa is a deity from Dahomey in West Africa. They are sometimes seen as separate entities, but also as a dual but single entity. These 'twins' are the Moon Goddess Mawu and Sun God Lisa. Part of the region's creation myths, they shaped how the world is today. So great were their powers that they asked Da the World Serpent to cradle and protect it.

As a perfectly complementary dual deity, they balance their energies. In some stories they are two separate entities. In these stories, after creating mankind, Mawu retires to the heavens, after a while watching her creations and realising things are not going as well as they should with them, Mawu sends her partner Lisa to teach them to clear areas as well as how to create tools so they could hunt and build.

Mawu is also regarded as the ruler and creator of human souls or "mawuse" (literally meaning the mawu within).

- Feast Day – There is no known feast day on which to worship them.
- Sexuality – Non-binary.
- Symbology – Clay, moon, sun, earth, flint spearhead.
- Crystal – African opal.
- Colours – White/silver and gold/yellow/orange.
- Vocation – The arts.
- Incense – Though nothing is known of, I like using African rose and myrrh.
- Altar – If you want to give offerings to Mawu-Lisa, create something at dusk or dawn to complement both aspects. Create a space in your garden/ balcony. Light a yellow and a white and candle, to represent the sun and moon. Sit down and, with putty or any other type of clay, compound and create votives of what you'd like to bring into this world. Offer them to Mawu-Lisa, asking for the energy to give them life. When you are finished, give thanks for their help.

Europe

The ancient realm of Europe was home to many different cultural societies. To the north were the Vikings of Scandinavia. Next door were the Germanic tribes. Within Celtic lore, little is known, as any form of LGBTQI+ has been wiped from history via Christianity. All we have are glimpses into their world through ancient Greek and Roman authors who tell of relationships and handfasting's. In Ireland's case, a great example would be to look at works by Piaras Feiritéar from 1600–1653.

IRELAND

The Emerald Isle has always had a rich tapestry of invasions and magic and mystical foundations that are still felt in its lands, in her castles, Fae mounds and monuments. Though we understand that handfastings could be held by a couple, this did not end here as anyone could enter into such a yearly partnership. Relationships were just as free and open here as those in mainland Europe and, indeed, as written about. As Ireland is awakening from its Christian slumber, these words are being addressed and acknowledged as it is breaking free of its shackles and EQUALITY is again taking centre stage.

Briged/Saint Brigid/Mama Brigantia

This goddess has well and truly spanned the globe. Though she is a Celtic goddess at home in Ireland, she travelled with her people via slavery and suppression to the Caribbean, becoming the only white Voodoo Loa.

A goddess of healing, fertility and fire, Brigid connects with femininity and masculinity. As a goddess, she was the only one to become a Saint, thus keeping her abilities for her devoted followers. Her sacred day was even kept, securing her as the beloved guardian of her land and people.

Her stories in early Christian times have her sharing her daily life and bed with another woman and nun, Darlughdach. They are well-loved and have a great many books written about them that are worth reading.

- Sexuality – Lesbian.
- Feast Day – St. Brigid's Day, 1st February.
- Symbology – Brigid's Cross, cattle, fire.
- Colours – Green, white, red.
- Crystals – Carnelian, pyrite, rose.
- Animal – Cattle, especially the cow.
- Plants – Dandelion, blackberry, rose.
- Incense – Cinnamon, willow bark, mugwort.
- Altar – The set up for an altar to Brigid can vary, depending on what you are asking for or seeking advice on. For instance, if you are looking for healing then stick to a green cloth and candles, and add rose quartz with an incense of dandelion and willow bark.

SCANDINAVIA

Norse culture is sadly similar in that only a few stories remain within the Sagas of homosexuality as part of society. Many of the Norse deities have a tendency (especially Loki) to shapeshift between male and female.

Loki

Loki was the child of a giant. He was the joker and trickster of the pantheon of Asgard. Loki is known as a shapeshifter who regularly changes into the form of a human female, as well as a mare giving birth to the eight-legged horse Sleipnir after being impregnated by the stallion Svaðilfari.

- Sexuality – Pansexual/bisexual (depending on how you see him).
- Feast Day – Common date in use is 1st April.
- Symbology – Horned helmet, two intertwining snakes, mistletoe.
- Crystal – Pyrite.
- Colours – Red, gold, dark green, black.
- Animals – Foxes, snakes, seals, salmon, horses, vultures, crows and hawks, amongst others.
- Plants – Mistletoe, dandelion, birch, haircap moss.
- Vocation – Mischief. Voicing truths that no-one wants to hear and speaking for those who can't speak for themselves.
- Incense – Mistletoe, dandelion, cinnamon, peat, dragon's blood.

- Altar – I find that Loki isn't that fussy on what is there but I do find that, however you decide to honour him, he is fond of a shot or two of Fireball whisky. In my experience, the more you work with Loki the more you start searching for the REAL truth behind people and situations. Loki gets a bad rap for being one of mischief but, as a black sheep myself, I find that standing up for others (whether that be in terms of race or sexuality, etc) is as good as creating an altar for him. Honour him by being the one who stands up when everyone else stays quiet.

Odin

Odin is in this book for a very good reason. Being at the head of Asgard, he is the chief god who, as one would think, would know everything or be allowed to know everything. As God of Magic, he learned the sacred magic of Seidr from the Goddess Freya. It was a form of magic predominantly practised by women. In stories, it is said that in order to learn from Freya, Odin dressed as a woman so that he could do so.

It is stories like these that should be instrumental in teaching others how to understand something by wearing or dressing like those that you wish to learn from. If the king of the gods can have the courage and strength to do it – we all can.

- Sexuality – Cis straight.
- Feast Days – 22nd April, Odin's Day. Also every Wednesday or "Wotan's Day".

- Symbology – Valknut, spear.
- Crystals – Amethyst, hawk's eye, Odin stones (naturally-holed) and K2 stone.
- Colours – Cobalt blue, red and black.
- Animals – Wolf, raven, Sleipnir his eight-legged horse.
- Vocation – War, death, wisdom, writing, magic.
- Incense – Sandalwood, fir, ivy, cedarwood, juniper.
- Altar – To set an altar up for Odin, I always like to lay a spread of runes on a blue cloth with a statue of a raven. He does like a drink, so if you are offering wine/mead or any other alcohol, raise a glass and hail Odin first and at the end.

GREECE AND ITALY

The rise of ancient Greece brought with it a large pantheon of gods and goddesses, some which had been reappropriated from other countries, due to migration. The Greeks were, when it comes to deities, very progressive, as the majority of them fit into the LGBT+ umbrella.

As Greece fell and Rome emerged, it took from Greece its bounty of deities, just changing their names. For each listed here, I have given both names.

GODDESS OF THE DAWN

Greek = Eos
Roman = Aurora

Eos was the sister of the Moon Goddess Selene and the Sun God Helios. Her role was to herald in her brother's journey by bringing in the first light of the day. As Eos, she was the favourite goddess of the famous female poet, Sappho of Lesbos.

As mythology and history do clash here, I am adding her to this list due to the modern context of seeing Sappho as lesbian and the island of Lesbos being the Greek home of lesbianism.

However you want to see her, as Aurora, the goddess was worshipped by both young virgin females as well as first time married women, perhaps leading to the nurture of her role as a goddess for lesbians.

- Sexuality – Cis.
- Feast Day – 11th June on the Roman calendar.
- Symbology – The chariot.
- Colours – Red, pink, gold.
- Crystals - Golden quartz, pyrite, gold.
- Animals – Two horses.
- Vocation – Goddess of the Dawn.
- Incense – Rose.
- Altar – To create an altar for this bringer of light, bring in a red cloth and add a few pink candles and either scatter with rose petals or introduce rose essential oil to the warmed-up candle.

For prayers, I would go to the poet Sappho herself and use her *Hymn to Aurora*.

GODDESS OF WISDOM AND WAR

G = Athena
R = Minerva

Athena was very different to her fellow deities on Mount Olympus. Unlike most of her kin, Athena mainly kept to herself. Yes, she did have relations – in history and art she's most known for being with beautiful young maidens, giving rise to the belief that she may have been lesbian BUT due to her lack of sexual dalliances, we would see her as asexual.

- Sexuality – Asexual.
- Feast Day – 1st July, Athena's birthday. This is also the first day of the Grecian New Year.
- Symbology – Olive trees, armour, helmets and spears. Her shield with the face of Medusa was known as the Aegis.
- Colours – Grey, royal blue, red, white, yellow.
- Crystals – Iolite, lapis lazuli, clear quartz.
- Animals – Owls and snakes.
- Vocation – Wisdom, intelligence, knowledge and crafting.
- Incense – Musk, patchouli, sage, frankincense, cinnamon, cedarwood.
- Altar – When setting up an altar to Athena, I find that using two grey candles helps to visualise her grey eyes. Adorn the altar with her sacred bird the owl and branches of olives. If you can't find an olive branch, olive oil will suffice.

Athena is a powerful goddess who is great to call upon to aid in study, for exams and learning of any kind.

> *"Hear me, daughter of Aegis-bearing Zeus, you who spy out all my ways, and who are with me in all my hardships; befriend me in this mine hour (statement here)."*
>
> – The Iliad by Homer.

GODDESS OF THE HUNT AND THE MOON

G = Artemis
R = Diana

Asexual, this goddess of youth and the hunt was worshipped by lesbians. Her sexuality can be seen being alluded to in her desire to never find a male lover, the love of her female companions and devotees, as well as in the story of Artemis and Calypso.

- Sexuality – Depending on how you see her, asexual/ lesbian.
- Feast Days –
  - 7th–8th April: Feast of Artemis.
  - 9th May: Feast of Artemis.
- Symbology – The moon, bows & arrows.
- Crystal – Amethyst.
- Colours – Silver and white represent virginity. Green and brown for the woodlands.
- Animal – Stags and dogs.
- Vocation – Hunting, wild animals, virginity, nature and childbirth.

- Incense – Will respond to any woody aromas, i.e. cedar, cypress, etc.
- Altar – Focus on which aspect of her you wish to call upon for help. For instance, an altar of silver and white for her lunar side. If you are going to use animal offerings, make sure they are naturally shed or sluffed. Working and caring for animals is a fantastic natural way to engage with her.

GODDESS OF LOVE

G = Aphrodite
R = Venus

Though not a lesbian herself, many homoerotic tales were attributed to her. She was referred to by the Greek poet Sappho of the island of Lesbos as the greatest ally of homosexuals and lesbians.

- Sexuality – Cis.
- Feast Day – 6th February.
- Symbology – The scallop, shell, myrtle, girdle, mirrors and roses.
- Colours – Red, aqua, pink.
- Crystal – Rose quartz, morganite.
- Animals – Swan, dove, swallow and the dolphin.
- Vocation – Love, pleasure and beauty.
- Incense – Vanilla, jasmine, ylang-ylang and myrrh.
- Altar – Place a mirror in the centre of a table, with two pink candles on each side. Scatter the altar with rose petals and light the sweet incense. Look to Aphrodite when you need to feel your self-worth.

APOLLO

G and R = Sun God

The Greek Sun God and twin brother to Artemis is said to have taken many lovers, both deities and mortals. One such story of many is the one of the god and beautiful Spartan prince, Hyakinthos.

- Sexuality – Gay.
- Feast Day – 9th February and 7th October, Pyanopsia
- Symbology – The lyre, laurel wreaths, bows & arrows.
- Colours – Gold, yellow, red and orange.
- Crystals – Boulder opal, topaz, obsidian.
- Animals – Swan, python, raven.
- Vocation – Solar god, music & poetry, healing, honesty.
- Incense – Amber, myrrh, clove, mugwort, cinnamon.
- Altar – The brighter the better. I have found that mirrors with gold candles on either end of the altar with a simple amber and myrrh incense works well. If you need to find the truth in the matter at hand, ask him to shine his light into the darkness. Apollo is also a wonderful deity to call on when in the depths of sickness, anxiety and depression.

> *"Lord Apollon, you know how to do no wrong; and, since you know this, learn not to be neglectful also. For your power to do good is assured* (your request here).*"*
>
> – Eumenides by Aeschylus.

BONA DEA

Bona Dea is known only as Roman, though may have been acquired from a minor Greek deity. Bona Dea is seen, via statues, as being a more mature female with snakes and cornucopias. Bona Dea is known as being very particular to sacred women's rituals and rites, with only the initiated knowing her true name.

Her initiates were able to offer blood sacrifice and drink the richer wines. For the most part, use of such a wine during ritual was most likely observing the sacred rites of womanhood. Though her followers were mostly female, she is known to have been a source of prayer to both women and men, including select male initiates. Because of this, Bona Dea is seen as an LGBTQI+ deity, accepting that (some) males too, though they may not ovulate, are one with the goddess and in her eyes seen as such.

- Sexuality – Cis/lesbian.
- Festivals – 1st May is the Festival of Bona Dea.
- Symbology – Bowl feeding two serpents, cornucopia.
- Colours – Unknown. Maybe go with red for blood.
- Animals – Serpents.
- Vocation – A goddess of chastity, women's fertility and healing, also a protector of Rome.
- Incense – There are no official notes on her favoured aromas, but one element that is forbidden is myrtle. As Bona Dea is the Goddess of Generosity, bring in elements that speak to you.

- Altar – As a vestal goddess, Bona Dea holds the rites of chastity, as well as fertility, so your altar setup will really depend on your position. If you are honouring your chasteness then keep a clean crisp white altar, with libations of ivy leaf expressing self-rule over yourself. If you are seeking help with fertility or honouring being a mother or embracing menopause, then delve into the reds. Bring out the wine or, if you prefer, milk and incorporate ivy leaves.

GOD OF WINE AND PLEASURE

G = Dionysus
R = Bacchus

Deity of all things enjoyable. With his insatiable desires, this god of orgies and the good life was either poly or omnisexual. In any artwork or story depicting him, he is always surrounded by young men and women and adorned (if not naked) with comfortable furnishings. Those around him are generally in some form of nakedness or disrobing.

- Sexuality – Omnisexual/polyamorous?
- Feast Days –
  o 1st–14th February.
  o 17th March: Roman Liberalia, honouring the God of the Vine and Rebirth.
- Symbology – Vine and fig leaves, double-handled wine goblets/glasses, thyrsos (pinecone crown).

- Crystal – Super seven, amethyst.
- Colours – Green, burgundy, black and purple.
- Animals – Lions, snakes, all wild cats.
- Vocation – Fertility, the theatre, wine and sexual desires.
- Incense – Fig, ivy, cinnamon, fennel, pine, frankincense.
- Altar – To call upon the God of Enjoyment, play with modern concepts. Give your altar a theatrical feel: velvets, candles and goblets with sweet-smelling incense. Feel free to change to other scents that you feel are more intoxicating to you.

"O Lord, with whom Eros the subduer
And the dark-eyed Nymphs
And rosy Aphrodite play, you who haunt
The high mountain peaks, I beseech you, come to me.
With kind disposition, hear and fulfil my prayer
(request here)."

Anacrean

GOD OF LOVE

G = Eros
R = Cupid

The child of Aphrodite was always going to be associated with sex and love. Though he isn't LGBTQI+ in general, all forms of sexual encounters were endorsed by this winged deity.

- Sexuality – Cis.
- Feast Day – 14th February.
- Symbology – Bow & arrow, hearts.
- Colours – Red and pink.
- Crystals – Fire opal, rhodochrosite, selenite.
- Animals – Doves, love birds.
- Vocation – Sexual attraction and love.
- Incense – Apple, rose, myrtle, frankincense.
- Altar – An altar to Eros should always be sensual. You may like to spray some favourite perfume in the air or burn some oil or incense. If you like candle magic, a great way to ask Eros for help is to use an apple. Cut a hole into the top, large enough for a pink or red candle. Either inscribe on to the candle the type of person you are looking for or write it on a piece of paper. Light the candle and let it burn down to the apple or, while burning, light your paper in the flame and then let the candle burn down.

HERMAPHRODITUS/APHRODITUS

Hermaphroditus was the child of Aphrodite and Hermes. Though this is where the term 'hermaphrodite' comes from, Hermaphrodite was named from half of his mother's name and half of his father's.

Hermaphrodite, like many children of the gods, wasn't raised by them. He was instead brought up on Mount Ida by a Naiad nymph as a boy. He grew up protected here until, at the age of fifteen, he started to venture out on his own to see the places around him.

It was on one of his trips that he ventured into the beautiful forest of Caria. Settling by a pool, he was greeted by the nymph Salmacis who was automatically overcome by this youth. After a few attempts at seducing Hermaphroditus, at which he constantly turned her down, she left.

Taking this moment to bathe, Hermaphroditus took off his clothes and jumped in the water. Salmacis returned and entered the pool again, being brushed off while trying to embrace him. In a final attempt and in her desire for the young boy, Salmacis made a plea to the gods to be forever part of the youth that, on answering her call, caused the two to become one.

As a modern take, this story can be seen as being not just about a youth developing one's understanding of their own sexuality, but also as a way to understand intersex or non-binary people.

- Sexuality – Non-binary/intersex.
- Colours – Softer palettes of colours.
- Crystals – Quartz, anhydrite.
- Animals – Butterfly, moth, sea bass,
- Vocation – God of effeminate, intersex and non-binary people. Marriage.
- Incense – When crafting an incense mix, create a balance of masculine and feminine herbs and scents.
- Altar – To call on Hermaphrodite's energy, it always helps to equally balance your altar with masculine and feminine colours, or you could use a trans flag, as the colours are already adapted. Silver and gold-coloured tools are evenly mixed.

Working with this deity is not only good for enhancing awareness and acceptance of one's sexual identity; they are also a great one to call on when entering into marriage. Use a mix of incense, items and colours that combine you both into one being. As a couple, being able to honour the differences but also the duality of your coupling enables a strengthened bond, i.e. the incense or the colours you choose here, you may also want to use them in your own handfasting celebrations.

GODDESS OF MAGIC, CROSSROADS AND SACRED TRAVEL

G = Hecate
R = Trivia

As a guardian, a keeper of light and protector of the lost, there is little wonder that this goddess has entered into the hearts of the LGBT+ community. As a goddess between worlds, there is a natural attraction to her, in which we find a kindred guide and mother.

The goddess's priests in her temple, the Semnotatoi, were gender variant – tying her worship strongly back to the earlier Sumerian/Mesopotamian deity priesthood of Astarte.

- Sexuality – Cis.
- Feast Days – 31st January, 13th August and 30th November.

- Symbology – Keys, dagger, torches, cauldron, crossroads, triple moon, gateways.
- Colours – Silver, purple, black and red.
- Crystals – Obsidian, amethyst, hematite, labradorite, serpentine, black tourmaline.
- Animals – Dogs, frogs, wolves, snakes, horses, crows, owls and black ewes.
- Vocation – The moon, magic, the crossroads, ghosts.
- Incense – Myrrh, cypress, saffron, mint, poppy, storax resin, mugwort.
- Altar – Devotees of Hecate will change certain aspects, depending on the individual rite concerned, but as a general honouring of the goddess, I like to stick to a black cloth, two red candles, one on either side of a statue of her and a silver bowl.

If you feel the need, dress the altar with some crow feathers and a key. You could always have a central candle which you could draw a key onto.

I wait at the crossroads Hecate.
Close my eyes to hear your voice,
To listen as you guide,
To see and feel the fires of your sacred lights.
Free me in my times of darkness,
Cast away those who cause me shadow,
I walk tall with you. I am brave.

GODDESS OF THE HEARTH AND SACRED FLAME

G = Hestia
R = Vesta

The Goddess Hestia was a sacred goddess worshipped in every home and building, with an effigy usually sitting on or next to the hearth. She is one of only three chaste goddesses (the others are Athena and Artemis).

Hestia is seen today as being asexual, as there are no stories of her being in relationships, as well as her being a goddess who demanded from Zeus that she would forever remain her own.

- Sexuality – Asexual.
- Feast Days – Vestalia is the 7th to the 15th of June.
- Symbology – The hearth and fire. Oil, wine, household instruments.
- Colours – Red, orange, yellow.
- Crystals – Garnet, sunstone, coal (not a crystal but does resonate with the hearth).
- Animals – Pig, donkey.
- Vocation – Goddess of the Hearth, Family and Domesticity, Architecture and the State.
- Incense – Hollyhock, goldenrod, chaste, yarrow.
- Altar – As the Goddess of Home and Family, Hestia is a great goddess to call upon if seeking help or protection for family members. An altar can be nice and simple with a white cloth and red candles.

Adorn the altar with images of the family or individual that you are asking her for assistance with.

Hestia, I find, is wonderful to help with individual building projects – anywhere from a simple goal to creating your actual home. Use symbols representing your project to call on her for protection and guidance.

GREEK GOD OF THE WILD

G = Pan
R = Faunus

Pan is known in many stories as having sexual relations with males and females. One of the most well-known stories is about Pan's relationship with a handsome young shepherd, Daphnis.

- Sexuality – Bisexual.
- Feast Days – 15th February: Lupercalia. 6th May: Shepherd's Day.
- Symbology – Pan pipes, musical instruments.
- Colours – Green, brown, tan.
- Crystals – Black tourmaline, smoky quartz.
- Animals – Ram, sheep, livestock in general.
- Vocation – Sexual awareness, protector of shepherds & livestock.
- Incense – Pine.
- Altar – Preferably go outside, into a park, backyard or forest, etc. The simpler the better. A log or a rock makes a great altar. You may like to add music to the atmosphere via your Spotify or other mobile

app. And, lastly, wine. Toast Pan with wine and leave a food offering to the wild creatures. After I finish, I like to give the rest of the wine as an offering by pouring it as a libation onto the readymade altar.

GOD OF THUNDER. FATHER OF THE GODS & GODDESSES OF MT. OLYMPUS

G = Zeus
R = Jupiter

The Greek Father of the Gods took more lovers than all of Olympus. Mainly known for his love of young women, he was also known for his love with the cup-bearer – the mortal boy, Ganymede. Paiderastia was a common practice in Greece, with its custom coming from this relationship. Men generally took on a young male, not just sexually but also as teachers of what was expected of a Greek man.

- Sexuality – Bisexual.
- Feast Days – Every Thursday. The Olympic Games. Zeus has many others but if you require accurate dates, please find a good ancient Greek calendar converter.
- Symbology – The lightning bolt, a sceptre, oak trees.
- Colours – White, red, gold.
- Crystals – Selenite, topaz (you may like any crystals with flashes of light in them that represent lightning).
- Animals – Bull and eagle.

- Vocation – Father of humanity, ruler of the sky and weather.
- Incense – Cedar, oak, orange, almond, hyssop, vervain, agrimony.
- Altar – As the god of gods, I like to keep his altar very austere. White cloth with gold candles and a statue of him.

India

ARDHANARISHVARA

In Hindu myth, when Parvati and Shiva inter-connected their bodies, they took on this androgynous form. Split right down the centre, their bond signifies the balance of nature and knowledge. Worshipped by many trans/non-binary and gender fluid devotees in India and Bangladesh.

- Sexuality – Intersex.
- Feast Days – Whenever you choose.
- Symbology – Trident and mirror.
- Colours – White and red.
- Crystal – Ruby.
- Animals – The bull of Shiva and the lion of Parvati.
- Vocation – Duality, fertility, spiritual fulfilment. Unity. Wish fulfilment.
- Incense – You can easily choose a nag champa, but try balancing masculine and feminine scents like rose and sandalwood to honour their duality.
- Altar – Create a nice simple dual aspect cloth, perhaps bringing in a red and a white candle. Add some flowers and symbols that represent duality to you.

BAHUCHARA MATA

Today in India and Bangladesh, this goddess of chastity and fertility is seen as the protector of the (old term) Hijra (eunuchs, trans and intersex) community. This third sex community of India has been around since long before the *Kama Sutra* (written approx. 400 BCE–300 CE), as they are mentioned in its pages.

Many of the stories of the goddess display sexual interchange. Her devotees strive to live a non-violence lifestyle.

- Feast Days – Koothandavar: 18 days in April and May, starting at the full moon.
- Symbology – Sword, nose-ring, trident, crown, red sari, flower garland.
- Colours – Red and black.
- Crystals – Garnet, ruby.
- Animal – A rooster: symbol of innocence.
- Vocation – Patron of the Hijra community, chastity and fertility.
- Incense – Saffron, musk, though a lovely jasmine and sandalwood can work well too.
- Altar – Dress your altar with a deep red cloth with black candles. You may like to add fresh flowers and a symbol of a rooster. Bahuchara is a wonderful deity to help anyone on their trans journey at any stage.

VISHNU/MOHINI

This creator god regularly took the shape of his female avatar, Mohini. Mohini became Vishnu's identity when covertly operating around demons to protect the other deities and or his followers. Today, Mohini is regarded in a modern sense by their followers as gender fluid. Many trans Indians give offerings to them/her.

- Sexuality – Straight, but as an avatar of Shiva can also be seen as trans.
- Feast Day – Fifth day of Brahmotsavam (look at a Hindu calendar for yearly dates).
- Symbology – Conch shell, sword, drinking bowl, the chakra disk.
- Colours – Blue, green.
- Crystals – Shaligram stones, emerald, peacock ore.
- Animal – Peacock.
- Vocation – Goddess of Enchantment Illusion or Deception. Seduction.
- Incense – Lotus.
- Altar – Set out a sweet-smelling space with incense, mirrors and candles, etc. As a goddess of enchantment and illusion, she/they are a wonderful deity to ask for help with feeling true to who you are, or to help give you that feeling of illusion until your journey is complete.

The Americas

The Americas, though diverse, share their sense of equality, with other sexes being happily embraced. From north to south; we have the first human couple in Inuit lore, who were both men and in order to have children, one was magically given a vagina. The Marine Goddess Sedna was seen in stories as either trans, lesbian or bi.

Traditionally, throughout the tribes of the Americas, the Native American two-spirit people were male, female, and sometimes intersexed individuals. These people combined the activities of both men and women, along with traits unique to their status as two-spirit people. In most tribes, they held a distinct, alternative gender status, with roles within the community being assigned on their preference. It is much in the same in the core beliefs of many Pacific Island nations.

CANADA AND GREENLAND

INUITS

Sedna

Sedna, also known as the Mother of the Sea, is a goddess of marine creatures and sea-dwelling mammals. In her many stories throughout Canada and Greenland, Sedna is generally seen as having a lesbian relationship and never wanting to marry. Inuits see her as both a negative and positive energy, just like the ocean.

- Sexuality – Bisexual/lesbian.
- Feast Days – 24th December to 7th January.
- Symbology – Mermaid, water, eye, fish.
- Colours – Aquamarine, blue, green, white and black.
- Crystals – Aquamarine, pearl, ocean-washed stones.
- Animals – All sea life, especially seals, whales and walruses.
- Vocation – Sea goddess.
- Incense – Willow, juniper, rosemary, sea salt, birch.
- Altar – I like to use a dark blue cloth, representing the ocean depths, and add a wide white candle. Crush your dry incense so it is ready to burn and then add it to your altar candle when it has melted in the centre enough that you can sprinkle small amounts onto it.

If you already have or want to keep a fish, why not call it Sedna to bring her energy flowing through your home. Working with her, anytime you eat fresh produce from the sea, always give thanks for what you are eating.

Asiaq

Asiaq was a weather deity that, although generally depicted as a goddess, was also occasionally depicted as a god. She/he was traditionally summoned by the medicine person of the village. She had the powers to change the seasons, but primarily was in control of the snow. Today, the Greenland weather survey group is known under her name.

- Sexuality – Trans/intersex.
- Feast Day – Unknown.
- Symbology – Snow.
- Colour – White.
- Crystals – Turquoise, lepidolite.
- Animals – Seals, deer.
- Vocation – Weather.
- Incense – Essential oil blends on a burner tend to work quite well.
- Altar – To invoke Asiaq, I find it best to go outside. Use a simple white candle and, if you want, some sweetgrass; or perhaps create a weather blend of oils to rub on your pulse points.

NORTH AMERICA

Within Native American tribes can be found stories of the berdache. Today, the word has been replaced with the term two-spirit.

As a separate sexual identity, they were those who took on the roles and functions of the opposite sex. Two-spirit acknowledges the multi-duality of sexuality in its many diverse forms.

There are some fantastic essays and books written by Will Roscoe on the subject that I will reference at the end of this book.

Earth Prayer
Hey! Learn to hear my feeble voice
At the centre of the sacred hoop
You have said that I should make the tree to bloom.
With tears running, O Great Spirit, my Grandfather,
With running eyes I must say
The tree has never bloomed.
Here I stand, and the tree is withered.
Again, I recall the great vision you gave me.
It may be that some little root of the sacred tree still lives.
Nourish it then
That it may leaf
And bloom
And fill with singing birds!
Hear me, that the people may once again
Find the good road
And the shielding tree.

Black Elk

Asgaya Gigagei – Cherokee

In Cherokee lore, the Spirit of Thunder is Asgaya Gigagei, also known as the Red Man or the Red Woman. When called upon by the shaman as a healer, they will generally appear as needed to the person being healed.

- Sexuality – Dual aspect.
- Feast Day – N/A.
- Symbology – Thunder.

- Colour – Red.
- Crystal – Desert glass.
- Animal – Thunderbird.
- Vocation – Thunder and healing.
- Incense – Yerba santa, sage, sweetgrass.
- Altar – Working with a spirit who is a powerful healer is a great chance to do some healing of your own. Whether it be for a friend or family member, group healing or sending energy to the earth, Asgaya Gigagei can be just who you need.

Before you start setting up, find some soothing background sounds of Native American drumming or, if you prefer, a soft thunderstorm on Youtube or Spotify. Create a healing space with a picture of the person, group, etc that you would like to send healing energy to. Light your sweetgrass and begin to focus on your task. I generally like to focus on the person in question and imagine their body being surrounded by blue lightning. I envision their body radiating light and becoming healed. Thank Asgaya Gigagei for their guidance and help.

The Great Spirit

The Great Spirit is a leading figure for ALL first nation peoples of North America. It is this epic force that breathes life into everything, teaches wisdom to those who listen and will help in spirit quests or journeys.

With over 570 recognised tribes in the US, there are many different names for the Great Spirit.

In the Cherokee belief structure, they call the Great Spirit Unetlanvhi. Unetlanvhi is not characterised as being male or female and does not have sexualised roles, but instead it is a true omnipotent being that is all-encompassing and created the earth for its children.

In Algonquian, of Quebec and Ontario as well as parts of the upper north of the US, its name is Manitou.

The Anishinaabe peoples of the Michigan area used the name Gitchi Manitou to refer to the Great Spirit, and the Iroquois people called it Orenda.

In Sioux belief this Great Spirit was called Wakȟáŋ Tȟáŋka and known as the Great Mystery. It is believed all creatures and objects on earth contain sacred spirits.

- Feast Days – Any day.
- Symbology – Go with your instinct. They are every-thing, so whatever you bring in their honour will work.
- Colours – All colours.
- Crystals – All crystals.
- Animals – All animals, but sit quietly and ask the Great Spirit to bring an animal that they wish to be with you.
- Vocation – Life, death and everything in between. All your dreams are their business.
- Incense – Choose incense or herbs local to you.
- Altar – The outdoors is the greatest altar you could be given. You don't need anything but your true self. Sit by a tree, a lake, or wherever you feel a connection to the Great Spirit and just close your eyes and ask for their help.

You breathe your first, I waken you.
Look to the land, you see me.
Listen to the babbling stream, you hear me.
A breeze sending goose-bumps on your skin, you feel me.
A blossoming flower's perfume, you smell me.
All that you choose to eat, you taste me.
Close your eyes at the end, we are again one.

Begochiddy – Navajo

Begochiddy is the duel creator deity in Navajo legend or Diné Bahane'. The story of the four worlds is an interesting one that shows the loving nature they have for humanity and every other creature placed here.
Sexuality – Dual deity. Trans.

- Feast Days – Any day.
- Symbology – Four, i.e. four discs painted the colours of the four worlds.
- Colours – Black, blue, yellow and white.
- Animal – All animals, though you may choose an animal in the myth.
- Vocation – Creator.
- Incense – Feel free to choose any, or you might like to use sweetgrass.
- Altar – Go out and find a place where you can be alone. You may like to paint four plates, symbolising the four worlds that Begochiddy created.

THE CARIBBEAN

In the Caribbean Islands of Haiti, Puerto Rico, Cuba, Dominica as well as in Brazil, the American South and also Louisiana and New Orleans, Voodoo is still widely practised under the name Voodoo(u) or Vodun.

The practice of Voodoo travelled by way of the French colonisation of this area from the French occupied nation of Dahomey (now Benin), where it was and still is practised by its population.

The slaves who brought Voodoo with them to the Americas still follow the same ideology; though have Christianised many concepts in order to practise their faith. Based upon one head deity and multiple spirits, it is one of the most LGBTQI+ friendly belief systems known, with a plethora of spirits who are openly LGBTQI+ or are helpful and welcoming towards the community.

Voodoo has many misconceptions, thanks to Christian missionaries and Hollywood BUT, contrary to popular culture, it's not all about ritual animal sacrifices. Like other faiths, there are many forms of practice, many of which can be standard rituals.

The spirits (Loa/Orishas) listed below are just an example of LGBTQI+ openness in Voodoo.

BARON SAMEDI – BI

In Haitian voodoo, Samedi is a deeply respected Loa (invisible and mysterious spirits) of all that is dead. He is generally represented in a black hat, black tailcoat, black pants (sometimes a skirt) and black sunglasses. He is a true dandy and very well put together.

As a spirit of the crossroads, he welcomes the dead to the otherworld. He has a fondness for ill children, who he would rather be called on to heal than see buried. He may also be summoned for house clearances, to remove unwanted or troublesome house ghosts.

Baron Samedi is seen as a rude, vulgar, fun-loving spirit with a filthy sense of humour and a love of very hot rum and cigars.

Seen within Voodoo as a Jesus-type entity, he is also a healer of illness as well as the one who makes sure the body has rotted in the ground to protect it from zombification.

- Feast Days – 2nd November is his day, but Saturday is a great day of the week to speak to him.
- Symbology – Coffins, skulls, bones, black sunglasses, the cross, the phallus, crossroads.
- Colours – Black, purple and red.
- Animals – Python/anaconda.
- Vocation – As Lord of the Dead, he commands and cares for all that relates to the realm of death, including graveyards and spirits. Ancestral wisdom. Guardian of the Crossroads.
- Incense – Tobacco leaf, black coffee and rum.
- Altar – To create an altar to the Baron, aim for setup on a Saturday. He loves toys and fun, so arrange it

as such. I use a skull and crossbones pirate flag for an altar cloth, have a piping hot cup of black coffee sitting as incense and also include some sexual innuendo. A dildo, vibrator or a banana shaped like a penis works well. If you have time (and aren't allergic!), create his favourite spicy rum with really hot peppers as an offering to him.

* Note: the rum you can always take with you to leave in a graveyard, if you don't like setting up an altar inside.

BARON LUNDY AND BARON LIMBA

I am purely placing these two on the list as they deserve recognition for their relationship together. As a couple, they taught a type of wrestling for gay men. There is not a great deal of information that I can find about them, but for gay relationships they can be a helpful couple to turn to.

ERZULIE DANTOR

Erzulie Dantor is a Haitian defender of women and is seen as a great protector. She loves all women and is always called on in cases of domestic abuse, to look after them. She is always seen with the darkest of skin, often being referred to as the Black Madonna.

- Sexuality – Straight.
- Feast Days – Tuesdays.
- Symbology – Pierced heart, knives.

- Colours – Gold, red, navy blue.
- Animal – Black Haitian pig.
- Vocation – Protector of woman, as well as defender of abused women and protector of lesbians. Finances.
- Incense – Florida water.
- Altar – A picture of the Black Madonna can be easy to find. Place it on an altar with a navy-blue cloth and either (or both) red and gold candles. If you wish, you could include two knives, representing her strength. Give your room a good healthy spritz of Florida water to help her come through.

GHEDE NIBO

Ghede Nibo was adopted after his violent human death by Baron Samedi and Maman Brigitte. He is generally depicted as an effeminate man in drag with a nasally voice. When he takes human form in Voodoo, his vessel is known to be highly sexual.

- Feast Days – November in general.
- Symbology – Bottle of medical herb-infused rum. A cross, representing the four elements. Cigars.
- Colour – Purple.
- Animals – Black rooster or black goat for sacrifice.
- Vocation – Death and healing. Guide of the dead, those especially who died young, violent deaths.
- Incense – Ginger, cedarwood and sandalwood.
- Altar – Ghede Nibo is a wonderful Loa to call on when you are wanting to send a message to a beloved person who has died.

ORUNMILA

Orunmila was the Orisha fortunate enough to see the very beginning of the world and gained the wisdom to foresee all mankind's futures. He cares for ALL humanity, regardless of sex.

- Sexuality – Cis.
- Feast Day – 4th October and Sundays.
- Symbology – Cowry shells, seeds.
- Colours – Green and yellow.
- Animals – Cats, dogs and snakes but loves all creatures.
- Vocation – Destiny, wisdom and addressing fate. Protector of humans.
- Incense – Though you can find what you need in the US and online, you can use basil, rosemary and other formulas that you prefer for cleansing and divination.
- Altar – A nice yellow cloth with green candles (or vice versa) does well. If I'm needing help in a hard situation or working with a difficult client then I like to place my deck that I'm working with on the altar, spread seeds over the cards and ask Orunmila for the ability to see clearly and to help plant the seeds for new ways of thinking within the client.

OSANYIN (YORUBA/SANTERIA/ CANDOMBLÉ AND/OR VODOU)

Osanyin is a forest Orisha, generally given the form of a shorter man with one eye, one leg and a walking stick, who is immensely knowledgeable and useful to anyone working with healing plants, mind-altering herbs and poisons. He is the creator of the Onisegun.

I have placed him here not for being of a particular sex but as a healer of all life forms, no matter their sexuality.

- Sexuality – Cis.
- Feast Day – 19th March.
- Symbology – He is often portrayed as a bird sitting on a metal staff. Beads, flowers, mushrooms.
- Colours – All colours.
- Animals – Birds.
- Vocation – The forests, healing herbs.
- Incense – This will depend on the motive for invocation, i.e. healing herbs, calmative, removing negativity, etc.
- Altar – As a healing altar, place whichever healing herbs that you choose on the table. If you are crushing herbs or mixing oils, have everything ready. As you prepare you concoction, ask Osanyin to guide your hands to heal the person in question. If it helps, write the name of the person on a piece of paper or have a photo and place it on the altar.

DAMBALLAH

In Voodoo, Damballah is an androgynous bisexual serpent or rainbow. Primordial, it is Damballah the great white/black snake that cradled the earth on its coiled body, creating the mountains and valleys with its movement.

From his creation, the weather was formed along with the first rains. The rains brought the first rainbow in the guise of the Rainbow Serpent, Aido-Hwedo. From that day to this, they are still in a loving relationship. Together they maintain order and balance.

Damballah is known for being generous and giving BUT it is recommended to invoke him only when you are truly in need of help.

As creator of earth, Damballah is a harbinger of peace, love, wealth and good health.

- Sexuality – Bisexual.
- Feast Day – 17th March.
- Symbology – The world.
- Colours – White or black.
- Animal – Serpent.
- Vocation – Love in ALL forms.
- Incense – Before trying to work with Damballah, make sure your space is free from heavy scents. So, if you're a smoker, you might air the place out, wash and wear clean clothes. An incense needs to be soft and light, so I usually just use a spray of orange blossom water.

- Altar – An altar to Damballah is lovely and simple. I generally keep two white candles with a large bowl of water for it, as well as a bowl of milk representing seamen and the milk of creation. If you wish, depending on what you are asking for, you could bring in other items that are white; i.e. rice, linen, flowers, etc.

ERZULIE FREDA

In Voodoo, Erzulie Freda is linked to love and all forms of sexuality. She is a flirtatious deity who, in ritual, when seducing a follower, doesn't distinguish them by their sex. Erzulie Freda is well known as patron of gays and lesbians.

- Sexuality – Pansexual.
- Feast Days – 15th September. Tuesdays and Thursdays of the week are good.
- Symbology – Three rings and a heart.
- Colours – Gold, blue, pink, lavender and orange.
- Animals – Horses.
- Vocation – Love, beauty, dance and jewellery.
- Incense – Rose, Florida water, orange, or any other fresh clean scents.
- Altar – As a deity of beauty and finery, it is important to make sure that her sacred space is clean and lavish. Spritz the altar space with Florida water to cleanse the area and give a sweet smell. I like to have a light pink silk tablecloth and lay three pink roses on the table with three rings and some pink

champagne (or prosecco) that I can give as an offering after asking for her help in love or business matters.

OSHUN/ERZULIE (YORUBA/SANTERIA/ CANDOMBLÉ AND/OR VOUDOU)

Oshun Yeye Iponda, Oshun Yeye Kare, and Oshun Panchagaye/Panchagarra is an Orisha who has many roles. Born in the freshwater rivers of Africa but at home in all fresh water, she is the essence of every stage of womenhood, as well as patron of love.

- Sexuality – Pansexual. A fluid goddess who is not trapped by any fixed sexuality but free to be what she is.
- Feast Days – 25th March, 8th September, and Saturday's.
- Symbology – Mirrors, fans, brass, fresh water, amber, mermaid.
- Colours – Yellows, coral.
- Animal – Mermaid.
- Vocation – Oshun cares for womanhood in all its stages and forms. She is a patron of prostitutes, gay and gender-variant males and gender-variant and lesbian women. Healing, prosperity, divination, magic.
- Incense – Use a most sweet-smelling incense. An oil diffuser/burner works well here.
- Altar – As an Orisha of freshwater, it always works well to have some in a bowl (you can water the

plants later). Lay out an altar with a mirror in the centre and some pieces of amber. If you wish to leave an offering to her, add a bottle of champagne/prosecco. Oshun is a gracious one to seek when you need strength and healing, or if you are wishing to study any form of divination.

OYA (YORUBA/SANTERIA/CANDOMBLÉ AND/OR VODOU)

Oya is a female warrior and a battle-ready Orisha originating from the Niger River. She is the mistress of the winds and storms. Her other interests are in traditional marketplaces (now shopping centres and businesses).

Oya is a wonderful Orisha to call on when you need to remove blockages, move on in your life, or need someone to walk with you in ancestor work.

- Sexuality – Pansexual. Like the wind, she is what she is, when she is.
- Feast Days – 2nd February, 25th November, and Friday's.
- Symbology – Masks, scythe, manchette, lightning.
- Colours – Burgundy, purple and brown are favourites.
- Animal – Water buffalo.
- Location – The marketplace and business matters. The wind, especially west. Cemetery gates. Patron of gender-variant, gay and bi men.
- Incense – Instead of smoke, use an oil diffuser with pine and other lovely flower scents.

- Altar – To set up a space for Oya, use a cloth of the above colours with candles and bring in some flowers. When making offerings to her, I like to use a glass of red wine or a freshly cooked chocolate cake as offerings. Like with all Orisha, it's a good idea to first choose which area you would like her to help with.

* Tip: You want the energy to be precise. Know what you want removed first. As Oya can make great changes

SOUTH AMERICA
MEXICO

Xochipilli

The Aztecs revered the Flower God Xochipilli as a protector of homosexuality and gay prostitution. In the lands ruled by the Aztecs, this god was a specific guide and protector of male prostitutes.

- Sexuality – Gay.
- Feast Day – Unknown.
- Symbology – Corn, flowers, Argrave, plants especially heliotropic ones, tobacco. A rattle.
- Colours – Unknown, although many paintings of him are in yellow, orange and red.
- Animal – Butterfly.
- Vocation – Homosexuality, prostitution, dance, writing and journeying into the other realms.
- Incense – Jasmine, pineapple sage, morning glory, St. John's Wort and rosebay willow. Any other herbs that bring you into an altered state.

- Altar – To call upon Xochipilli, set up your altar to be as cheerful and lively as possible. I tend to use orange, yellow or red candles. Arrange a bowl with flowers currently in bloom or bring in some ears of corn. I like to adorn mine in bright colours. If you have a rattle or anything that makes music you can play it while you have the incense going to change consciousness (if you don't, try to get some gentle native music to help connect). Relax and invite him to enter your space.

Awaken from your slumber, arise from your cocoon.
Stretch your wings, your clothes of light.
You are renewed, show the world who you are.
Fly, flutter, dance with me.
You are my people.
For you....
I'm always here.

AZTEC

Ometeotl = Ometecuhtli/Omecihuatl

Ometeotl is the dual creator deity of Aztec culture. They are both singular and plural in nature and they split mainly to give birth to the Aztec pantheon, as well as ALL life on earth.

As a religious figure who represents the understanding that everything has an equal and an opposite, Ometeotl becomes a relevant deity to understand sexual awareness in the Aztec empire.

- Sexuality – Intersex/trans.
- Symbology – Maize.
- Colour – Any but use light and dark.
- Animals – Any that you feel drawn to.
- Vocation – As a creator of all, Ometeotl can be called on for anything.
- Incense – To create a blend, use an equal mix of masculine and feminine scents; i.e. jasmine and cedarwood.
- Altar – To set up an altar to this creator being, I like to try to balance everything, so there is an equal harmony of light and dark, silver and gold tones, etc. Showing an understanding that everything has to have an opposing force is a great way to acknowledge their creator aspect.

Xochiquetzal

With a name meaning 'flower bird', Xochiquetzal is one of the oldest of the Aztec pantheon, giving birth to many, but also seeing the birth of the other deities and humans. Though she is ancient, she is immortally youthful and loves anyone who dedicates their life to making beautiful things as well as making others happy, especially prostitutes.

Though she was married to the God of Water, she was also a consort to the chief creator god. She loves sex, pleasure and happiness.

- Sexuality – Straight.
- Feast Day – Atama Quilaztli (Harvest Festival) is celebrated every eight years.
- Colours – All bright colours.
- Animals – Birds and butterflies.
- Vocation – Weavers, crafters, fertility, lovers, and is also a guardian of prostitutes.
- Incense – All intoxicating floral scents can be used, the more sensual the better.
- Altar – Feel free to make this altar as beautiful as you can, with mirrors, feathers, flowers, etc. Though traditionally she did enjoy the sacrifice of a beautiful youth; perhaps instead seek her favour by weaving a bracelet or creating anything else to offer her.

MAYAN

Chin

Though not much is formally known about this dwarfish stout god, he is recognised as bestowing gay relations within the Mayan people. It is documented by the head Christians that it was a standard practice that pre-wed teens as well as elders took male youths as sexual outlets. These youths were seen as wives so much so that if one was taken, they would have to be compensated for.

- Sexuality – Gay.
- Colours – Go with your gut instinct.
- Animals – Panther, toucan, or whichever animal you feel connected to.
- Vocation – Gay relationships.
- Incense – Palo santo.
- Altar – As extremely little is known about Chin, it falls once again to your own deeply personal feelings. The animals that I connect with here have connotations of beauty, grace, self-belief, strength and joy. Palo santo is a very intoxicating and oddly sensual South American incense that you could mix with other scents which link you and your partner. Add to your altar items belonging to you both and ask Chin to help with strength and endurance in your relationship (hence the panther), as well as much joy, happiness and love (hence the bright colours of the toucan).

AN A-Z UNDERSTANDING OF SEXUALITY - SCIENTIFIC AND MEDICAL DESCRIPTIONS

The meanings of many terms that describe sexuality have been listed in many dictionaries, as well as on-line. Although they have no emotional connection attached to them, they *are* necessarily laden with subtle and often loaded meanings for many people who are trying to understand their fellow humans. Some terms are still, sadly, used in an insulting manner. In a world where we are developing our sexual identities ever more, this list is not intended to be a static one but rather it will grow as society's understanding of its sexual selves likewise grows.

- Aromantic – A person with no desire for a romantic relationship.
- Asexual – A person without sexual feelings one way or the other.
- Bisexual – A person who loves and can have a sexual relationship with either sex.
- Cisgender – Relates to anyone who perceives their personal identity and sexuality to be associated with the gender allocated to them at birth; i.e. a man assigned to a man's body. Opposite of transgender.
- Drag – A person who dresses up to entertain.
- Gay – A word used to describe male homosexual culture as well as a man who loves and/or has sex with men.

- Gender-fluid – A person who doesn't see themselves as a fixed gender.
- Intersex – A person who has both male and female sexual characteristics or body parts. A person inbetween traditional concepts.
- Lesbian – A woman who loves women and/or has sexual relationships with women.
- Non-binary – A person who is more androgynous in gender and sexuality.
- Omnisexual – An individual who is attracted to persons of all genders and orientations. The term is often used as a synonym for pansexual.
- Pan-romantic – A person who is romantically attracted to people of all sexual orientations and gender identities.
- Pan-sexual – A person who, whilst in a relationship, doesn't consider gender identity, biological sex or gender.
- Polyamorous – A person who can be in many different sexual relations at the same time, all of which are consensual.
- Queer – The American group Queer Nation introduced this as an umbrella term for all LGBTQIA+ people, but please note that some people still consider this to be a derogatory word and, for this reason, it is best to check that the person to whom it is being applied is accepting of its application before using it.
- Sapiosexual – A person who finds intelligence sexually attractive or arousing.
- Straight – A person who only has relations with the opposite sex to them.

- Tomboy – A girl who exhibits characteristics or behaviours considered typical of a boy; for example, wearing masculine clothing, preferring more physical games and interests.
- Trans female – Allocated as a male at birth, but identifying as female.
- Transgender – A person who does not consider their sexuality and their birth body as compatible.
- Trans male – Allocated as a female at birth, but identifying as male.
- Transsexual – A person who considers that they belong to the opposite sex, both physically and emotionally (this term is going out of use and was traditionally applied after surgery. This term is more likely to be used by older people, as a reference for themselves, to describe the medical change to their true self).
- Transvestite/cross-dresser – A person who enjoys wearing the clothes more usually associated with the opposite sex.

AN A-Z UNDERSTANDING OF SEXUALITY THROUGH THE EYES OF THE LGBTQIA+ COMMUNITY

An entry in a dictionary can only ever offer a limited and descriptive explanation of a word that is being used to communicate an emotion or aspect of sexuality; it cannot convey a definitive account that also fully covers all the nuances of the feelings associated with the word.

Members of the LGBTQIA+ community were asked to provide their own meanings and understandings of some of these terms. It is hoped that these more personal responses will provide a better understanding of the human aspect of each term.

Within the many responses and suggestions received, I had a difficult time deciding which ones to use here as, with many, I was lucky enough to have four or five to choose from. I'm thankful to everyone within the LGBTQIA+ community who chose to respond and make this section possible.

Aromantic – *'I've never felt that romantic spark with anyone. In a relationship I've never felt the desire to be lovey, hold hands, etc. I can still have a loving relationship with someone that others might see as platonic, but that context isn't there.'*

Asexual – *'For me, there are feelings of sensuality, but these do not arise from other people. I feel that sex is a mechanical act, whereas sensuality comes from my relationships with the natural world around me. My Paganism is rooted in the heart, in plants and trees. An unfurling leaf is sensual in texture, shape and smell; shells and stones have a power to move me deeply. I have never felt the same with a human being.'*

Bisexual – *'To me, I think I fall into the bisexual category. I love women as much as I love men; the difference for me is that, if I'm in a relationship, I stay within the boundaries of our relationship. Meaning, if I'm dating a man, I am with him only; if I am with a woman, I stay with that woman. In my eyes, I am open to love in all forms.'*

Cisgender – *'I am a male born in a male body, and I'm happy and comfortable in the body that I'm in.'*

Drag – *'I use drag as an entertainment, to over-emphasise aspects of myself, create a character, and be able to do and say things I would never have the confidence to do in my day-to-day life.'*

Gay – *'I realised I was sexually attracted to men quite early on, so I have never thought of females in the same way. Being in a same-sex relationship is just natural to me; I never thought of it as anything else.'*

Gender-fluid – *'I feel a bit of a shapeshifter. Though, in my case, it tends to be a more gradual build up. I can relate as he/him for months and then slowly morph into more she/her. I don't personally fully change how I dress but I allow flexibility in my broad wardrobe. I know a few friends who like to really dress how they feel, but I'm not comfortable enough for that.'*

Intersex – *'Though I was born a boy, I've never really fitted into that role. As a teenager, I really struggled to identify with anyone, as I would be bullied for my feminine features and mannerisms. There was a time when I thought about transitioning, feeling that physically being female would be better all-round, but I've grown to accept and understand ME on ALL terms. I am straight. I am effeminate, but my DNA is what it is.'*

Lesbian –
(* Note: this response is from a couple, hence why the quote is written both in singular and plural)

'To me, being a lesbian means that I am a woman who loves a woman. I love a woman who looks like a woman. If I wanted to date someone who looked like a man, I would date a man! But I get that we all find different people and looks attractive. I can appreciate a good-looking man but wouldn't feel a physical attraction in the same way. We often say, "I'd stand him in the corner to look at!" The good thing is that as we both find women attractive; we can acknowledge our appreciation of them without getting in trouble with the other! We are both secure in our relationship and love for one another. Being in a lesbian relationship doesn't mean there has to be a "butch one"! We both possess quite a lot of men's clothes – but this is mostly because we both like the styles and

in fact it's mostly women who ask me where I got them. I like to think I wear them in a womanly way. I don't try to look like a man. We both have long hair. I wear it up, down or half and half. We rarely wear makeup but I might do if I'm going out somewhere. I don't like the word lesbian. I don't really know why – I just don't like the sound of it. I will often use gay as a generic term if I need to use a label. I tend not to use labels anyway – if someone asks me if I'm gay then I say, "no I'm (name)!" Or in conversation, I may refer to my wife – and expand on that if I need to. I see people as just the name they use and who they are....not an age, gender or sexuality, etc. To be honest, those things don't really go through my mind when I meet or interact with someone.'

Non-binary – *'A lot of people think that being non-binary is about rejecting the concept of gender. I don't see it that way. For me, being non-binary is about embracing all of the spectrum of gender. I don't specifically identify as male or female, and I do not think that either really applies to me, because I feel like I have stepped back and can see both as two halves of the same whole. I can recognise aspects of what people might traditionally label as "male" and "female" within myself, but I do so in the knowledge that these aspects are not separate or opposed to one another. They are all parts of the same whole. I might have a day of wearing sparkly jewellery and baking cakes, but I am still not "female" on those days. Similarly, when I wear "masculine" clothing, I am still not "male". I am all genders.'*

Omnisexual – *'I've just always been drawn to who I'm drawn to. I am happily aware of my individual partners' identities but I've never seen that as a hindrance. I see each of my experiences for the sexuality and person they are.'*

Panromantic – *'I can experience both romantic attraction and sexual attraction with someone, regardless of their gender. Some folks like to split between the two aspects.'*

Pansexual – *'To me, being pansexual means being attracted to people, regardless of their gender. And to me, that fits with my experiences and how I feel. It does not mean that I'm likely to be unfaithful with anyone who walks by, and it does not mean I love my husband any less because I can experience attraction to a wider range of people than he can.'*

Polyamorous – *'Polyamory in summary is a term for ethical non-monogamy where you can love more than one person at the same time. Not all connections will be the same, but consent is the key to it being ethical. All parties consent and have knowledge of other partners. How this is expressed depends on the individuals. Some people have a closed triad and may even live together. I personally identify as solo polyamorous, as I chose not to go down the traditional route of relationships and chose not to live with a partner or get married. This could change in the future but currently I have one partner in Scotland who I see every week and chat with on the phone, and a long-distance partner who lives in*

Devon, and we try to see each other every few months. All our relationships are open to others too. Also, how we interact with what is called a metamour (meaning a friendship with your partner's partner), depends on the individuals.'

Queer –
(* Note: what follows is a variety of both positive and negative responses to try to communicate the vast differences that exist regarding the use of this term)

'Growing up, "queer" was not a term I was abused with, so I realise that I lack a certain emotional response associated with its use.'

'For me, queerness encompasses my sexual identity as someone uncomfortable with binary presentation. It also encompasses my rebuke of cisgender and heteronormative privilege. LGBTQIA+ labels tend to presume a binary origination, and their usage coincides with a social movement that seeks assimilation and erases the existence of non-binary identities. Using "queer" as a catch-all umbrella term, whether intentionally or not, silences that important fringe voice.'

'I loathe the word with every fibre. As from a child through till the end of university that term made my life hell. Constantly picked out, yelled across the field at me. It got to the point if something comes on the TV with the title "Queer" I turned the channel off. The word holds every memory of pain, fear, hurt and sorrow I grew up with.'

'I realise that the word is being "empowered" in a different way but a word of hate will always be a word of hate to a vast swathe of the community.'

Sapiosexual – *'I can happily say that I am attracted to people based more on their personality and intelligence – which takes many forms, it's not just academic intelligence.'*

Straight – *'I'm a cisgender woman who has only ever fancied men. I'm not attracted to all males, I'm really rather specific in my tastes, but women just don't do anything for me.'*

Tomboy – *'In my opinion, "tomboy" is a word for a female whose interests defy outdated gender norms, whether it's hobbies, interests, professions, or anything like that. I don't think anyone under a certain age is called a "tomboy" anymore because those "boy's must do this, girls must do that" days are behind us.'*

Trans female – *'Even as a child, I never thought of myself as a boy. I was always happiest playing with my female neighbours and friends than with boys. I tried to hide within my born body at school by being sporty, but hiding brought on severe depression. After leaving school, I finally took the step to become a female through hormone therapy and surgery. I am now living how I always knew I was. The person who I see in the mirror is the lady that has always been inside.'*

Transgender – *'I was born a male and never felt whole. During my 20s and 30s, I would dress up in female clothes and became friends with transvestites, wondering if this was the answer. I realised in a short period of time that this was still not being true to me. Dressing up was just that. I was feeling like it was putting a band aid over a deep cut. It did however help me realise that to be true to myself I needed to transition and become a full female. I've been a female now for 20 years and have never felt more complete and content within myself.'*

Trans male – *'For me, the transition from a female body to a male body has meant becoming my authentic self. Having been born in 1958, I had no knowledge, no access and no support in finding out why I felt "off" in myself. Moving to Europe enabled me to learn how I could join my inner and outer selves to finally become whole. What an amazing feeling! It saved my sanity!'*

Transsexual – *'Being transsexual, in my eyes, is knowing from very early on that you were born in the wrong (gender-wise) body. Thinking patterns and preferences also usually follow the brain's idea of said trans person's gender. It's funny actually, because while I'm definitely trans male, I'm most definitely bi. I appreciate beauty and intellect, no matter what package it comes in.'*

Transvestite/cross-dresser – *'Being able to dress up on a night out, or to go out dressed, isn't about believing I'm born the wrong sex, but more to experience life as my partner's sex, as well as gaining a sense of freedom from being someone else.'*

Epilogue

I wanted to take this journey of world culture through the eyes of the rainbow community. Initially this is to show that we have always been here and always will be. However, this led to years of making new friends with new deities and discovering, that as society has changed, we have lost so much freedom and love along the way.

Along this journey, it has been a source of joy to see certain symbols appear again and again – in particular, the rainbow and the snake.

The rainbow appears in almost all creator myths, while those creators are either androgynous or widely accepted as trans. It is in itself a wonderful link to a new spirituality of the original Pride flag created by American gay artist Gilbert Baker, who was also known under her drag name as Busty Ross.

The second symbol of the snake can now be viewed in a different context. In Abrahamic scriptures, it is the snake that causes the expulsion of Adam and Eve from Eden. We can perceive the snake as the possibility of Lilith getting her revenge, or we could see the apple in itself being sexual desire (forbidden fruit) as Lilith tempting Eve and Eve succumbing to her.

The snake can also be seen (again in a different context) as not just a Pagan symbol suggesting that the story St. Patrick was actually trying to show was through teaching Christianity to the Irish, he banished not just Paganism but other sexualities by removing all traces of them from ancient stories and 'modern literature'.

If this book does nothing else but to pique your curiosity into a particular culture, belief or a single deity, then I'm happy to have bridged that gap. If it leads to a wonderful journey of self-study and years of reading, then I'm ecstatic. This was never meant to show and teach everything, but rather to bring the world to you and give you the road map to discover a new journey for yourself.

For those who wish to read further, there is a treasure trove of books available on myths and legends from around the world. With some stories, like those from Hawaii, Greece and the Philippines, their folklore is open and sexualities are easy to see. Others definitely take a bit of prying. Don't be discouraged. Dig deeper.

This world once contained so many gods and goddesses who once represented us. If called on again, they still do and will always. We have always been part of the tapestry of humanity. Let's bring that back and re-emerge from the darkness.

Thank you for sharing this journey with me.

TOM.

Reference Guide

Eliade, Mircea – *Australian Religions* (1973). Ithaca, Cornell University Press, pp. 113–114.

Sears, James T. – *Youth, Education and Sexualities: An International Encyclopedia* (2005). Greenwood Publishing Group.

Murray, David A.B. – "Who is Takatāpui? Māori Language, Sexuality and Identity in Aotearoa/New Zealand" (from *Anthropologica*, Vol. 45, No. 2, pp. 233–241) (2003). Canadian Anthropology Society.

Westervelt, W.D. – *Hawaiian Legends of Volcanoes* (1916). Boston, G.H. Ellis Press.

Von Scott, Steff – *From Ishtar to Eostre* (2023).

Peled, Ilan – "Assinu and Kurgarru Revisited" (from *The Journal of Near Eastern Studies*) (2004).

Brouwer, Hendrik H.J. – *Bona Dea: The Sources and a Description of the Cult* (1989).

Bruchac, Joseph & Caduto, Michael J. – "Four Worlds: The Dine Story of Creation" (from *Native American Stories*).

Grimal, Pierre – *The Dictionary of Classical Mythology* (1996). Wiley-Blackwell. p. 209.

Conner & Sparks – *Cassell's Encyclopedia of Queer Myth* (1998).

Tinsley, Omese'eke Natasha – *Ezili's Mirrors: Imaging Black Queer Genders* (1971).

Dayan, Joan – *Erzulie: A Woman's History of Haiti* (1994).

Herskovits, Melville J. – *Dahomey: An Ancient West African Kingdom* (1938), 2 vols. New York.

Jones, Grant D. – *The Conquest of the Last Maya Kingdom* (1998). Stanford U.P.

Miller, Mary & Taube, Karl – *The Gods and Symbols of Ancient Mexico and the Maya: An Illustrated Dictionary of Mesoamerican Religion* (1993), 1st edition. Thames and Hudson.

ACKNOWLEDGMENTS

Special thanks to Steffy V. Scott for your valued knowledge.
Thank you Suzi Edward Goose for the cover artwork.
Facebook: @artworkofsuzi-edwards-goose-inkwitch
Instagram: inkwitch333

Tom Lanting is an Australian-born Pagan and author who lives in Edinburgh, Scotland with his husband.

Tom has been a member of the Scottish Pagan Federation council serving as its LGBTQIA+ Officer for over 9 years. He is part of Gemini Aspect with his husband Iain, who is a master wand-maker and cloak specialist.

In 2021, with the support of the Presiding Officer of the S.P.F. at the time, Tom created the first officially registered Pagan Tartan. His first book was *Scottish Paganism and LGBT+ Sexuality*.

9 781915 580252